Is Kindness Killing the Church?

Letters to seven twenty-first century churches

Hugh Osgood

malcolm down
PUBLISHING

First published 2023 by Malcolm Down Publishing Ltd.
www.malcolmdown.co.uk

26 25 24 23   7 6 5 4 3 2 1

British Library Cataloguing in Publication Data
A catalogue record for this book is available from the British Library.

ISBN 978-1-915046-56-7

Cover design by Angela Selfe

Art direction by Sarah Grace

Printed in the UK

Dedication

To my fellow church members
– from those who prefer to sit at the back
to those who faithfully serve at the front –
a thought-provoking look at the unity of the Church,
advocating greater engagement and
an openness to more robust problem-solving.

Contents

Foreword

I came into my post as general secretary of Churches Together in England just as Hugh Osgood was completing his two terms as the Churches Together Free Churches president. Hugh and the other CTE presidents had not had an easy time helping Churches Together in England navigate its way through some polarising issues.

Like Hugh, I have been deeply touched by those denominational leaders who speak of coming together to learn from one another, but have observed that some find it easier to learn *about* others rather than to learn *from* them. To go forward we have to engage, convinced that unity involves proceeding together.

In this book, Hugh argues that we must proceed on the basis of truth as well as grace. He sees securing everybody's engagement in discussions about truth as vital, if the truth about unity itself is to be upheld. For him, narrow visions of unity that shut down debate are as unhelpful as wider visions of unity that see working through discord as a distraction. He has written very graciously to address such tendencies at a grassroots level, believing that the voice of every church member can help to bring change.

His argument for both a robust and deeper level of unity is timely, and is surely the only way forward for a Church that yet again is having to cope with pressures from the very society it seeks to transform. Twenty-first-century issues may differ from first-century ones but the Church that faces them still needs to confront them with a unity that works rather than falters.

So this book is an invitation for individual Christians, church leaders, Church denominations and indeed interfaith networks to deepen a sense of the kind of Church needed for the twenty-first century. We don't need a homogeneous Church, but rather one that through the work of the Spirit becomes the best version of itself as it works in unity with others.

I have admired the ministry of Hugh Osgood over many years. The Churches in Communities (CIC) church network that he founded represents one of the most vibrant growing Church movements here in the UK and beyond. I have been grateful on a number of occasions to glean his wisdom and reflections on the ecumenical journey in England, and this book represents not only his passion to see the Church flourish but also for the Church to undertake timely self-examination to assess honestly and self-critically where we are at.

I commend Hugh as a writer, thinker, theologian and senior church leader. I commend this thought-provoking book. I trust you enjoy your journey of finding a more perfect way for your church and a re-prioritising of Jesus' imperative in his prayer to his Father, that 'they ... be brought to complete unity' to let the world 'know that you sent me and have loved them even as you have loved me'.[1]

Mike Royal
General secretary
Churches Together in England

---

1. John 17:23.

Introduction: Letter to the Reader

Is kindness killing the Church? That really is a risky question, especially as in Church circles kindness is so highly prized. Obviously, nothing will kill the Church, as Jesus has declared he will build his Church 'and the gates of Hades will not overcome it'.[2] But kindness can be suffocating as well as subtle, and although we know that it will never completely stifle the Church's life, there is a sort of kindness that can seriously hinder the Church's progress. Let me explain.

A few years ago, despite having engaged in the world of inter-church relations for many years, it dawned on me that I still struggle to understand how the current approach to Church unity is supposed to work. When I committed my life to Christ in my teens, I was very happy to live almost entirely in my own sector of the Christian world. So it came as a surprise when God started to impress on me that it is going to take the whole of his Church to impact the whole of his world. I was not sure how to respond. How could the various parts of the Church be properly brought together, and what kind of unity could speak to a sceptical world?

I had been around long enough to know that when the world claims that our disunity is the cause of their dismissiveness, it is just an excuse. I realise that if we were to become a monolithic organisation speaking out with monotonous predictability the words the world wants to hear, we would probably be just as easily marginalised. I think we have to accept that being a provocation to the world is more important than seeking its preferment, and that being a lively Church held together by love and respect will definitely have something to say to a world where violence, disrespect and dismay so often hit the headlines. But there was something in me that was beginning to realise I was being taken on a 'wait and see' journey, as if I might not know just how much

---

2. Matthew 16:18.

impact a rightly relating church would have on the world until the right relationships were actually in place. I needed to press on and trust God for the outcome.

The first thing God had to show me was that, with some adjustments, all the parts do actually fit. I was sceptical about this at first as all I could see were people engaged in trying to assemble a jigsaw puzzle where the picture on the lid seemed to have been lost. On top of that, it appeared that a number of the pieces had not only become misshapen but had developed the ability to back away from the very connections they needed to make to complete the puzzle. Not that this seemed to be deterring the would-be assemblers. They were handling every piece with care, as if trying, very politely, to persuade each one to fit where it was never meant to be. I do see this polite, well-meaning mispositioning as part of a pattern of kindness that is increasingly paralysing the Church.

With this concern in mind, and the words 'they do all fit' still lodged in my brain, I began to see the importance of considering a fresh approach. While I wholeheartedly believe that only God can reshape any misshapen pieces and counter any tendency to disconnect, I am convinced that he has already given us the picture that we need in order to assemble the pieces correctly.

This, then, is what this book is about – offering a picture and giving some clear pointers on how the pieces, with God's help, might be able to come together. And so as not to be too ambitious, I am beginning by offering my pointers at a local level.

So, just to give some clues as to where we are heading, let me say a little more about my convictions concerning the picture, the fit and the possible adjustments. Central to all three of these is my understanding that when Jesus prayed for unity, as recorded in John 17, he was actually asking the Father to seal the reconciling work he was about to accomplish on the cross. He was most definitely not setting some far-off goal for the Church to aspire to. He was absolutely securing then and there the unity that was to be the very hallmark of the New Covenant relationships that would come into being through the giving of the Holy Spirit. This being the case, we should be living out our God-given unity in all the robustness of the unconditional love that the Holy Spirit brings. This has to be liberating.

Without wanting to be too negative, the problem with seeing unity as a goal rather than as a given is that we end up feeling uncomfortable with the unity we have, and start struggling to create a kind of unity that was never intended. It is hard to know if the theology built around a claim that the John 17 prayer remains unanswered is a cause of this struggle or a consequence of it. Either way, perpetuating the thought of a unity yet to be accomplished runs the risk of some churches passively waiting for the prayer to be fulfilled and in the meantime disengaging with others. At the same time other more unity-minded churches will feel obliged to work towards a unity of their own imagining where a warm but bland politeness can easily become the order of the day.

Sadly, in chasing a dream that constantly fails to be fulfilled, whole sectors of the Church are being tied into a long-running guilt trip. We need to be free to gather confidently around our different opinions, without apologising for having them; to enjoy some hard-hitting debates while affirming the things we have in common; and, within measure, to be looking at our inter-church history with fewer regrets and a greater willingness to celebrate the things we can learn from it.

Grasping this concept of every piece of the Church having been raised up to fit will be the first challenge for many in considering the approach I am about to advocate. The second challenge concerns the picture we need to have before us.

In the final chapters of the Bible, we see at one and the same time a picture of the Church as a bride and as a city. Combining those in our mind's eye is beyond us, so we can be grateful that it is the city picture that dominates. We see in Revelation 21 and 22 walls of truth, founded on the teaching of the apostles. We recognise wide-open gates, through which the river of life carries leaves from the tree of life to heal the nations. We see transparency in streets of gold, and we revel in the blazing light of God's presence that removes the need for a temple and guarantees that darkness has gone forever.[3] So there we have it – the picture of the Church that one day will most definitely emerge, and the stronger we hold to that image in our hearts, the sooner we will see it. Abraham held on to that city picture and left Ur to look for it.[4] King David held onto it and sought to build its earthly counterpart.[5] We are now closer to its full manifestation than either of them ever was.[6] Even so, we have to be realistic.

In writing to the Ephesians, the apostle Paul instructed them to 'make every effort to keep the unity of the Spirit through the bond of peace',[7] while a few verses further on he wrote that God's people need to equip one another 'until we all reach unity in the faith'.[8] So what is the current picture that we now have to hold in our heads alongside the ultimate one we must hold in our hearts? In other words, what does it look like to keep the unity of the Spirit while pressing on to the unity of the faith?

Well, I believe it looks exactly like the Church in the New Testament. Its members accepted that they were one in the Spirit and yet were prepared to put a lot of effort into confronting their differences, but they did not dilute their passion even when they had to agree to differ. For them, passionate disagreement was preferable to a vague and unsatisfactory compromise. There was a relational oneness built initially on the unity Jesus created among his strikingly diverse band of twelve closest disciples. It reached new heights on the day of Pentecost, when

---

3. Revelation 21:1 – 22:5.
4. Hebrews 11:8-10.
5. Psalm 46:4-6; 48:1-3,12-13.
6. Hebrews 11:39-40.
7. Ephesians 4:3.
8. Ephesians 4:13.

3,000 new believers were empowered alongside the initial 120.[9] It was a unity that endured persecution under Saul of Tarsus and extended into Samaria, Phoenicia, Cyprus and Syria.[10] Ultimately it was the unity that carried the Church onward to establish congregations throughout the known world.[11]

That first-century unity is exactly the same unity that God has given us today. It is still capable of handling straight-speaking debate and is secure enough to hold us together as we impact the world at large. I honestly believe that it is possible for every part of our twenty-first-century Church to match the momentum of the Church in the New Testament. I see this possibility as creating a great interim picture of the ultimate unity we must embrace.

Throughout this book I will be keeping that first-century picture before our eyes, convinced that the outworking of the gift of the Spirit in the first-generation Church should be (and should always have been) the pattern for the outworking of the gift of the Spirit in every expression of the Church in every generation since. I realise that this thought could also be a challenge for some. I do, however, have one more challenge in store and it is an even more direct one, relating to the adjustments that may be required, and it will take us back to the book of Revelation. Not this time to chapters 21 and 22 but to chapters 1-3.

Before us we have seven golden lampstands, five of which have flickering flames. These represent the seven churches that existed at the end of the first century in what is now the Aegean region of Turkey. Among them stands the One who not only declared himself to be 'the light of the world'[12] but also proclaimed the same over his Church. As we read what Jesus goes on to write to these churches, some of us might throw up our hands in horror. 'Has it come to this – the story of the

---

9. Acts 2:1-41.
10. Acts 8:3-4; 11:19-20.
11. Acts 1:8.
12. John 8:12.

first-century Church ending in lovelessness, compromise, immorality, deadness and apathy?' Others may say, 'Hold on. We have been taught that these seven churches are symbolic of seven periods of Church history and we can now ignore churches one to six as we are in the Laodicean age with the world showing all the negative trends of the last of the last days,[13] and a global Church that must be making God sick.'[14]

I don't want to dismiss these views lightly, but I do see value in reading these Revelation verses differently. For me it is significant that we see seven very different churches with very different needs and yet Jesus has not stepped away from any of them. It makes me equally determined not to step away from fellow churches today, no matter how compromised or pressurised they might be. I value the fact that Jesus brought a corrective to the five whose flame flickered, a corrective designed to bring them back on track. To read the seven letters he went on to write to them as condemnatory preludes to every church's downfall is exceedingly short-sighted. Why not presume that the diagnoses and prescriptions that he offered actually worked? After all, what church today would be unwilling to submit to a direct treatment plan from Jesus? Why should we expect anything less from churches that were so much closer to the momentum released on the Day of Pentecost?[15] Some of the believers in the seven churches would have remembered Paul teaching in the School of Tyrannus,[16] and all would have known John, who had lived among them until he was deported to Patmos.[17] It would not have been hard for them to recognise what they had been robbed of by their waywardness. Being told how to get back on track would have been welcome news.

But there is a particular reason why I want us to adopt a positive attitude to these seven churches – not just towards the two that needed

---

13. 2 Timothy 3:1-5.
14. Revelation 3:16.
15. Acts 2:1-47.
16. Acts 19:9.
17. Revelation 1:9.

no correction. I know that if we are serious about fitting together in line with God's image of unity, many of our churches today will find themselves welcoming their own mid-course correction. I am not going to be so presumptuous as to claim we can find the exact words that Jesus would use to make this happen, but he did tell each of the seven churches to 'hear what the Spirit says to the churches' (plural).[18] This shows us that although churches have to address their own problems, they can be good listeners, compassionate encouragers and good prayers into other churches' situations.

Sadly, in my experience, churches often have more insight into each other's problems than they have into their own. Unfortunately, this usually leads to disconnections rather than stronger engagement, so we have to tread carefully. On balance I think disconnection may have been a significant contributing factor to the Revelation churches' problems and that the exhortation to 'hear' was part of their prescriptions. A good way forward for us today would be for our churches to become capable of speaking to one another in love, sharing their insights into each other's situations in readiness to having their own circumstances spoken into. This, in some ways, is what we are about to do in the chapters ahead, but we will be adopting a number of safeguards.

Firstly, we will be writing letters to seven stereotypical churches that represent congregations, regardless of denominational affiliation, that we might find in any of our towns and cities today. We will be doing this by imagining that the leaders of the seven Revelation churches, once restored, are still with us and can speak together into the circumstances of these congregations. In effect, their imagined corporate voice will be answering the question, 'What would the seven churches in Revelation want to say to our seven stereotypical churches today?'

The second safeguard is that in our writing we will aim to be honest without being judgemental. When Jesus declared that the gates of

---

18. Revelation 2:7,11,17,29; 3:6,13,22

Hades would not overcome the Church,[19] he would have had in mind the invasive strategies of the enemy, as in ancient times the gates were where elders sat to formulate their city's plans. Paralysing the Church is high on the enemy's agenda. He may now no longer speak against us in heaven where Jesus has ascended to be our advocate,[20] but he does accuse us here on the ground.[21] He accuses us to ourselves and to others, and accuses others to us. But he has not been cast down to punish us but for us to punish him. Our assignment in God's plan of redemption is to overcome the accuser even as the accuser seeks to overcome us. And the book of Revelation tells us that we do this 'by the blood of the Lamb', 'the word of [our] testimony' and by not loving our lives so much 'as to shrink from death'.[22]

In his first letter John wrote: 'If we walk in the light, as he is in the light, we have fellowship with one another, and the blood of Jesus, his Son, purifies us from all sin'.[23] At the same time as the enemy is trying to paralyse the Church by inducing apathy and unreality, he is also seeking to undermine it by introducing animosity. We must resist the temptation to believe his lies, thinking that we have gained new levels of discernment. We have to walk together in the light, as sinners saved by God's grace, forever willing to lay down our lives for him and for each other. Our words will need to reflect this, being neither words of apathy nor animosity.

The third safeguard is that once we have the letters from the seven churches, we will read them out loud, just as the leaders must have read the letters to their congregations in the first century. This will be an unusual experience as we have become so used to reading things and processing them personally that our responses are often very I-orientated, making

---

19. Matthew 16:18.
20. 1 John 2:1.
21. Revelation 12:10.
22. Revelation 12:11.
23. 1 John 1:7.

it easy to miss the point. In New Testament times, reading letters aloud to all who were assembled would have been standard practice and all would have jointly shouldered the responsibility. It would have been an engaging experience as people at times would have nodded their heads and grunted in agreement, while at other key moments they would have shaken their heads and tutted out of concern. And the engagement would not have stopped when the reading was over. It is humbling to know that although each one of us can play our part in progressing God's plan, none of us alone is going to be the whole answer.

With all this in mind, here is the list of churches that we are going to be writing to (and being stereotypical each church will begin with C):

- the Conciliatory Church
- the Conforming Church
- the Comprehensive Church
- the Curious Church
- the Concerned Church
- the Courteous Church
- the Confident Church.

Although I have to acknowledge that all of this must sound as if I am setting us up for an impossible task, there is one big factor that should make it easier. In order to give ourselves and our imagined Revelation church leaders some context, we will be writing the letters at key points in a narrative that covers some of the joys and challenges of the New Testament Church. As we break into our historical account by creating appropriate pauses, we will see how the lessons learned by the early Church are relevant for our churches today.

I realise that there will be a temptation within this approach for each of us to concentrate on the stereotypical church we reckon to be most like our own, but there is real value in having as many of us as possible appreciating the beauty and diversity of God's greater plan and thinking on behalf of others as well as for ourselves. So please resist the temptation to prioritise, and engage as widely as you can, remembering that although we can think on behalf of others, we cannot act for them. We need to hold onto Romans 12:18, 'If it is possible, as far as it depends on you, live at peace with everyone.'

In coming together to create the peace that God has on his heart, we can only contribute what we are responsible for. God's peace will always involve a combination of grace and truth. He is not interested in a patched-up peace that glosses over realities. Without everyone's contribution, the challenges we must wrestle over will never be properly resolved. So, as we read what needs to be said, we must trust that others will be reading too, and will also be responding by engaging appropriately.

To summarise, increasing engagement is high on my list of reasons for writing. Across our diversity we have a God-given unity that should help us grow, but it will only facilitate growth if we engage with each other wholeheartedly. Stepping delicately around one another as we seek to negotiate our differences will surely frustrate the Church and its mission. Going back to our title, overly cautious negotiating is the sort of 'kindness' we have to avoid. Strength was a characteristic of the Church in New Testament time – strong convictions, strong commitments and strong arguments, all existing side by side. Kindness had its place, it always has, but without wholehearted engagement it risks reducing the Church to a state of lukewarm vagueness.

Putting it bluntly, can we honestly afford to dilute the strength and power of Christian love or seek to downgrade a congregation's zeal to make them 'more acceptable'? Should we really back away from one another just because we fear we may intimidate them, or might put them off with our strongly fought arguments? Isn't it time to realise that on occasions when we believe we are being kind we could actually be coming across as patronising? Admittedly, this is most likely to occur when we are engaging too superficially, either by assuming overcautiously that a gap is too difficult to bridge, or by insensitively presuming that there is no gap to bridge at all. But is such assuming and presuming right? I can see that all of these things: the dilution, the downplaying, the withdrawing, the superficiality, the presumption and the patronising (which I really believe occur) can be well meant and have their roots in kindness, but it is a kindness that lacks the robustness of wholehearted engagement.

I really can understand how easy it is to think that everything can simply be brought together by patient positioning rather than by accepting that the pieces probably need some restoration. I can also see how, with no clear picture in mind and perhaps a conviction that we are working towards a unity Jesus prayed for but we have yet to achieve, it becomes a hope to hold on to. However, I know we can do better. I have said that looking back to the Church as it originally was can provide us with a clear picture that will help us portray the Church as it will ultimately be. I know that it can also help us with our piece-by-piece restoration. Eventually, as restoration takes hold across the Church, albeit at different rates, I am expecting that we will find as much encouragement from looking around as we can from looking back to the original or on to the ultimate. Momentum generates momentum.

So finally, by way of encouragement, I think that throughout Church history, God has been repeatedly seeking to bring about restoration through mid-course corrections. Undoubtedly the biggest mid-course correction was the Reformation, and even with that the pace and extent of change has varied. We are now 500 years on and rethinking is still occurring. Some churches that restructured half a millennium ago are continuing to see new expressions emerging. Others are still working at it little by little. Perhaps it is fortunate that not all of God's shake-ups are as seismic as the Reformation with its ongoing aftershocks. Smaller shake-ups are happening all the time and we need to be grateful that God is constantly acting to bring each piece of his picture back into the shape he intended it to be. I trust this book will help us welcome the shake-ups that are bound to come and to make the most of every God-initiated mid-course correction.

It is my hope that you will really enjoy the chapters that follow and find yourself increasingly drawn in as you head towards the ultimate picture. And, by the way, the characterisations of the stereotypical churches are designed to raise a smile rather than a frown.

Now, if we are set, let us begin in the upper room as the evening leads on to the John 17 prayer.

1. Disparate Choices

It's the night of the Passover Feast and Jesus has gathered the Twelve in an upper room.[24] The atmosphere is informal. As they chat together ahead of the meal, Jesus keeps things light, just as he has done so often since he recruited them. There are some long-standing friendships among the Twelve and some close family ties, but the group is not exactly well matched.[25]

Left to their own devices they might never have got on at all. Matthew, who collected taxes for the Romans, would not always have seen eye-to-eye with Judas or Simon the Zealot, both of whom would have wanted the Romans gone.[26] The age range is quite wide too, and so is the spread of their social backgrounds. Peter is a little older, a married man who has been running a two-man fishing business with his brother, Andrew.[27] John, on the other hand, is much younger, and he and his brother, James, are a more privileged pair. They have helped in their father's fishing business where much of the work is done by hired labourers.[28] Digging a little deeper, Andrew has the benefit of his friend Philip joining him.[29] Nathanael, on the other hand, who has been recruited by Philip, is probably left, like Thomas, to forge his own relationships in the group.[30] I guess if we had been putting the team together, we would have matched up people more carefully, but that never bothered Jesus. His personnel skills relieved tensions and broke down barriers, holding the team together despite their differences. Whether the Twelve realise

24. Matthew 26:17-20; Mark 14:12-17; Luke 22:7-14; John 13:1-2.
25. Luke 6:12-16. Bartholomew is called Nathanael in John 1:45.
26. Matthew 9:9; Luke 6:13-16.
27. Mark 1:29-31; Luke 4:38-39.
28. Mark 1:20.
29. John 1:44.
30. John 1:43-51.

it or not, they have spent three years being moulded together by the commitment, good humour and graciousness of Jesus.

But the atmosphere changes when Jesus gets up from the meal to collect a towel and bowl.[31] I used to think he was just making up for a routine courtesy that the householder had forgotten, but I now see it as far more deliberate. The lesson he is teaching is a major one, going beyond showing that cleanliness can be restored once the dust of a day's journey has been washed from our feet. In some ways that lesson is not new. He has been doing that for the Twelve figuratively ever since they met him. The way he debriefs with them at the end of each day is always refreshing. But now, as Jesus moves from one to the other, Peter, ever the one to go to extremes, bluntly asks for his head and hands to be washed too.[32] As Jesus assures Peter that this is not necessary, it opens up the topic for the evening: Jesus is going away and it is time for change. They now need to do for each other what Jesus has been doing for them.[33] They will have to find a different way to hold the group together.

It is not going to be easy. With Jesus in charge every member of the team is valued. Peter's bluntness is somehow blended in, and even the occasional displays of high-handedness by James and John are coped with.[34] Thomas' tendency to be sceptical is not a problem, and the list could go on. Jesus can deal with people's weaknesses as well as celebrating their strengths. There have been times when he has rebuked them, especially Peter, James and John, the three he has drawn closest to him, but he has rarely exposed any of their shortcomings publicly.

Unbeknown to the others, he is certainly aware of Judas' money-handling deficiencies,[35] and who knows what we might discover if there were recordings of their private conversations? Right up to this final

---

31. John 13:3-7.
32. John 13:9.
33. John 13:12-17.
34. Luke 9:51-56; Matthew 20:20-30; Mark 10:35-45.
35. John 12:6.

meal, Jesus has made sure that Judas is accepted unquestioningly by his fellows. Now things have to change. It is obvious that if they are to value each other as much as Jesus values them, a massive dose of graciousness will be needed. Losing some of their rough edges will help, but Jesus loves them with his eyes wide open, seeing all their defects. That is a kind of loving they have yet to discover.

With the bowl and towel back in place, it is time for them to face reality. Jesus speaks of a betrayer, and they look at each other, wondering who it could be.[36] Until now, grace has covered things, but they cannot stay blind forever. Going forward, a tougher kind of love will definitely be needed. But the changes they are about to see individually, and as a group, are only part of God's plan. He is going to change his dealings with the whole world in a way that will affect their generation and every generation to come.

To understand this global change, we need to leave John's account of the upper room and briefly turn to those of Matthew, Mark and Luke. They record how Jesus announces the change. John, on the other hand, moves from the foot-washing and departure of the now exposed Judas straight on to Jesus explaining what the change means. According to Luke, Jesus begins the meal by saying, 'I have eagerly desired to eat this Passover with you.'[37] In sharing this, Jesus could simply mean that this meal has been on his mind for all three years of his public ministry. But it could even have been in his thoughts since he planned redemption with the Father and Holy Spirit in eternity-past. For now, we will just go back 1,400 years to the introduction of the Passover Feast through Moses.[38] God would have known then that the meal that marked the start of the Old Covenant would also mark the start of the New Covenant that was to surpass it.

36. John 13:21-22.
37. Luke 22:15.
38. Exodus 13:3-7; 23:14-15.

Jesus makes the announcement at the critical moment in the feast when he breaks the bread and takes the cup. As he does this, he declares that his body will be broken like the bread and his blood poured out like the wine.[39] It is this self-sacrifice that will usher in the New Covenant – a freshly established, binding agreement, securing God's future dealings with humanity.

At this point we may need to get up to speed with some Bible knowledge the Twelve might already have known. As we have implied, the New Covenant was not a new idea. It was always God's plan. The rituals and regulations brought in under Moses were preparing for it, and when the Jews were exiled in Babylon, both the prophet Jeremiah and the prophet Ezekiel set out what a new covenant would mean. Jeremiah quoted God as saying 'The days are coming ... when I will make a new covenant ... I will put my law in their minds and write it on their hearts ... they will all know me, from the least of them to the greatest.'[40] Ezekiel recorded God's words as, 'I will remove from you your heart of stone and give you a heart of flesh. And I will put my Spirit in you and move you to follow my decrees and ... to keep my laws.'[41]

At the time of the exile, no one realised the extent of the intervention God would have to make for all of this to come about. What is more, even if they had known how much it was to cost, they would have found it hard to understand how widely it would apply. It was the prophet Joel who spelt out the breadth of God's plan: 'I will pour out my Spirit on all people ... and everyone who calls on the name of the LORD will be saved.'[42]

So, going back to John's record of the upper room, we find Jesus teaching around the four major New Covenant themes: knowing God, obeying God, having hearts of love and receiving the Holy Spirit. The

---

39. Matthew 26:26-28; Mark 14:22-24; Luke 22:19-20. 1 Corinthians 11:23-26.
40. Jeremiah 31:31-34.
41. Ezekiel 36:26-27.
42. Joel 2:28-32.

24

early part of the conversation is quite fragmented as the Eleven seem to skip over key statements made by Jesus as they pursue their personal concerns. As he shares his excitement about leaving so he can once again be glorified with his Father, Peter becomes agitated over Jesus going where he cannot follow.[43] It is complicated by the fact that Jesus knows he will be going away and coming back to them on two separate occasions. He will be going to the cross where they cannot follow, and yet he will see them again when he has risen from the dead. After that he will be ascending to his Father, where they will eventually follow, but in the meantime he will be sharing his life with them through the Holy Spirit. Peter, unaware of this two-fold pattern, promises to follow Jesus anywhere, even if it means laying down his life for him. In reply Jesus calmly predicts Peter's denial,[44] but seeing Peter's pain moves on quickly to speak of the place he will have ready for them when they eventually join him in his Father's house.[45]

Thomas and Philip then bring their questions, opening the way for Jesus to re-emphasise his oneness with the Father and to confirm that 'no one comes to the Father except through [him]'.[46]

Having established that within the New Covenant there really is a way for people to know God personally, Jesus has to engage with Judas (not Judas Iscariot, but the other disciple with the same name) who asks, 'But, Lord, why do you intend to show yourself to us and not to the world?'[47] Jesus answers him with his ascension and the giving of the Holy Spirit in mind. He and the Father will come, by the Holy Spirit, to those who love and obey him.[48] Jesus knows that the love and obedience they will need in order to receive the Holy Spirit will be theirs once they have been truly reconciled to God through his self-sacrifice.

---

43. John 13:36.
44. John 13:37-38.
45. John 14:1-4.
46. John 14:5-11.
47. John 14:22.
48. John 14:23-24.

But the Twelve are struggling to put it all together. There has been so much to take in since the foot-washing began to shift the responsibility onto their shoulders. Somewhere in the midst of it all Jesus has even given them a new commandment: 'As I have loved you, so you must love one another.'[49] This sets the bar even higher than 'love your neighbour as yourself'.[50] The good news is that Jesus has also given them this amazing promise, 'By this everyone will know you are my disciples, if you love one another.'[51] The fact that Jeremiah and Ezekiel promised that the New Covenant will bring new hearts that are set to keep God's law, definitely transforms this command into a promise. What greater proof could there be that we are Christ's disciples, living in God's New Covenant reality, than to be humbly showing new levels of love, and demonstrating our obedience?[52]

They sing a hymn and step outside, ready to make their way to Gethsemane.[53] As they walk, they are hoping that all this restructuring will begin to make more sense. The atmosphere outside seems calmer. They feel at home walking and talking with Jesus. This way of learning has been such a big part of their lives for the last three years.

As they pass a vineyard, Jesus talks about their future unity. The vine with its small stock and long, carefully tended branches provides a perfect illustration. Just as the vine and the branches are one, their continuing oneness with him will be what makes them fruitful.[54]

With the Kidron Valley ahead of them, Jesus continues to teach them about the Holy Spirit. He says it will be better for them to have the Holy Spirit within them than for him to stay alongside them. He wants them to know that just as he and the Father are one, so are he and the Holy

---

49. John 13:34.
50. Mark 12:31.
51. John 13:35.
52. John 14:7-31.
53. John 14:31; Matthew 26:30; Mark 14:26.
54. John 15:1-8.

Spirit. As they are his disciples, once they enter into their New Covenant relationship with him, they too will be one with him and the Father. This means that anything they ask of the Father in his name they will receive. The downside to this oneness is that those who hate him will hate them too, and yet the Holy Spirit will always be there comforting and strengthening them, guiding them into all truth.[55]

It is most definitely transition night and Jesus is holding nothing back. He wants them to have his life and love, and also his joy and peace. He tells them they are about to be scattered but they will come back together and their joy will be complete. He looks on them fondly and affirms that he has told them these things so that in him they might have peace: 'In this world you will have trouble. But take heart! I have overcome the world.'[56]

As they try yet again to take it all in, they are grateful that Jesus told them in the upper room that the Holy Spirit will remind them of all he has taught them and lead them into all truth.[57] But then, hardly missing a breath, Jesus lifts his voice and seals all he has said to them as he prays openly to his Father. He does this with a freedom that will soon be theirs. He has given them a pattern prayer,[58] but now he is giving them a pattern for praying. He has regularly sought out his Father to talk to him in secret but he has never held back from talking to him in public,[59] and he does so now with a confidence that his prayer will be answered. He knows that all he has talked about will shortly come to pass, so he prays the words that so many since have believed have ended up in our pending tray, 'that [they] may be one.'[60]

For the eleven who were listening, this is not a prayer being pointed in their direction. They have heard Jesus pray to his Father before and

55. John 15:6 – 16:31.
56. John 16:32-33.
57. John 14:26; 16:13.
58. Matthew 6:9-13; Luke 11:1-4.
59. Luke 10:21-24.
60. John 17:21.

know that this is not the way he treats these moments. He is happy to be heard so they can see his heart but he is not manipulative. In hearing the prayer, they become assured that somehow the New Covenant oneness Jesus has just been speaking to them about will soon be theirs.

We who have come to 'believe ... through their message' should have the same assurance. Better by far to live in the unity God has given in answer to this prayer than to try to cobble ourselves together into a unity of our imagining. Let's pause and take note:

My prayer is not for them alone. I pray also for those who will believe in me through their message, that all of them may be one, Father, just as you are in me and I am in you. May they also be in us so that the world may believe that you have sent me. I have given them the glory that you gave me, that they may be one as we are one – I in them and you in me – so that they may be brought to complete unity. Then the world will know that you sent me and have loved them even as you have loved me.[61]

Let's now take a moment to reflect on some key points that we can take forward:

- Jesus told them to wash each other's feet. What might this have meant to them figuratively going forward?
- Over three years Jesus had created a oneness between the Twelve that they were going to have to maintain. What would exposing Judas have taught them about maintaining unity?
- Jesus going away, initially to the cross and then to heaven, was a major theme in the upper room. Why would this have made the disciples anxious?

---

61. John 17:20-23.

- During the meal, Jesus mentioned the New Covenant. What do you see as the main differences between the Old Covenant established by Moses and the New Covenant brought in through the death and resurrection of Jesus?

- Aspects of the New Covenant had been set out by Jeremiah and Ezekiel after Judea's Babylonian captivity. How do the promises they referred to relate to the work of the Holy Spirit promised by Jesus in the upper room?

2. Letter to the Conciliatory Church

As we prepare to consider our first letter, we need to define the first of our stereotypical churches – a Conciliatory Church. In almost every town and city we will find at least one church that more than anything else wants to get on well with everyone. Let us imagine a town where Station Road Chapel is that church.

Station Road has a small, elderly congregation, some of whom are very enthusiastic. One long-standing member of the chapel, Ray, who is now retired, uses his organisational skills to make the most of the premises for the community. Ray is not fazed by the fact that they have to share their minister with four other churches. He sees himself as the minister's right-hand man and is happy to make sure that Station Road is very much on the town map. He even attends all the local inter-church gatherings and ministers' fellowship meetings on her behalf. He is amiable enough but can be a little impatient with churches that have a different agenda, particularly when he is looking for additional volunteers for some of the lunch clubs that Station Road runs. His approach is quite straightforward and he has often been heard to say that the gospel can be preached without words.

Those from Station Road who work alongside Ray may not share his enthusiasm for expressing his views but are more than happy to share plenty of words with those they meet through their community programmes. Everyone who comes into the building is welcomed at face value and conversations can focus on anything the visitors may want to speak about. Some of those hosting are not shy to invite people to the Sunday service at Station Road, describing it as a pleasant fifty minutes together followed by tea and biscuits. They assure everyone they will find a warm welcome and they are right. Many at the chapel have known each other and their families for years and relationships between them are very close.

When Ray shares his frustrations over some of the other churches in the town, as he does from time to time, the other members of the church have been around long enough to know many of the people who attend them. They quietly agree with Ray that it would be good if all the churches had community programmes as strong as theirs and everyone could simply lay aside their differences and get on with serving the community together.

When Ray has news of inter-church gatherings, they are happy to attend but mainly if there is a strong social element. In fact, they have become a little bit unsettled by the news that their own minister may be moving on and they could end up with someone who wants to put more expectation on midweek meetings for study rather than socialising. Station Road is a church that knows what it likes and it claims to like everybody. It is happy to come together with other churches at a level where everyone just gets on pleasantly with each other and aims to do the same with all those around them.

The statement from the upper room conversation that is most likely to register with a church such as Station Road is that 'everyone will know that you are my disciples, if you love one another'.[62] A stereotypical Concilliatory Church will stand out as a church that is firmly focused on building caring and friendly relationships within its congregation, and works hard to do the same with the community that surrounds it. It will be a church that is good at winning friends, and is successful at influencing people in authority. It will gladly engage in inter-church forums, even though it will back away from anything that their fellow churches are embracing that society might consider controversial or could lead to confrontation. Its clear preference would be for churches to present a united front in a way that would win society's approval. Obviously, a Concilliatory Church would like to see a unity that is centred on love.

---

62. John 13:35.

Now I realise that we are interrupting our first-century narrative very early on in order to address this church, but I think we have gleaned enough about the way Jesus expected relationships to change within the New Covenant to offer something helpful by way of a mid-course adjustment from the leaders of our now presumed-to-be-restored Revelation churches. Looking back to the letters they received from the risen Jesus, we know that none of them started at the level to which five of them fell. They had been well established by Paul and had had John living with them. They may even have been the first to read John's Gospel, and among the first to read Luke's. The words of Jesus in the upper room would have been familiar to them and John would have made sure that they would have known the new commandment that Jesus had given: 'As I have loved you, so you must love one another.'[63] John would also have made certain that they understood the unconditional nature of the love Jesus was speaking about. This would have made it all the more painful for the Ephesian church when Jesus told them that they had 'forsaken the love [they] had at first' and had fallen a long way as a result.[64]

It may be hard to think that there could be parallels between the Ephesian church and our Conciliatory Church today (whether it be Station Road or a church that is somewhat different), but the concluding story in John's Gospel should give us pause for thought. We know from our summary of the upper room conversation that there was to be a period of time between the resurrection and the coming of the Holy Spirit. It is during this time that early one morning Jesus meets seven of the Eleven on the shore of Lake Galilee.[65] After breakfast, Jesus takes Peter for a walk along the water's edge. Peter's three predicted denials now meet with three opportunities to recommit.

As they talk, Jesus deliberately uses two different words for love – one is *agape*, the unconditional love that the Holy Spirit can bring, and the

63. John 13:34.
64. Revelation 2:4-5.
65. John 21:1-19.

other is *phileo,* which is more akin to being affectionate. Jesus asks Peter twice if he loves him with unconditional love (*agape*). Each time Peter, in all honesty, because the Holy Spirit has not yet come to bring him that unconditional love, replies that he is affectionate (*phileo*) towards Jesus. The third time that Jesus asks he very graciously uses 'affectionate' (*phileo* instead of *agape*). This takes the pressure off Peter and leaves him anticipating the unconditional love that he is to experience a few weeks later when the Holy Spirit comes.[66] The difference between *agape* and *phileo* could be said to mark the extent to which the Ephesian church had fallen.

In coming to Christ, the Ephesian believers had known an initial passion they should have held on to, and it is sad to see how quickly things can be left or lost.[67] In the case of the Ephesian church, it had happened in less than four decades. In our eyes they were virtually a first-generation church, possibly with some original members still in place. This, for us, may make their lapse seem all the more surprising, but we cannot use longevity as an excuse for any lack of passion in our churches today. In some ways, there should be no such thing as a second, third or fourth-generation church. The Church that was birthed on the day of Pentecost ten days after the ascension was to be the template for every church in every generation.[68] Obviously church styles will reflect current local cultures, but the core message of life and love must never be changed. In generation after generation, the Church should know and show the vibrancy of the Holy Spirit. In looking back to its own beginning, the Ephesian church might have realised how close it came to missing out.

The Ephesian church was birthed some twenty-five years after the giving of the Holy Spirit at Pentecost (which our narrative is currently

---

66. Romans 5:5.
67. Revelation 2:4.
68. Acts 2:39.

leading up to), and its first twelve members presented Paul with a problem. On first meeting them he discovered they were gathered together on the basis of John the Baptist's ministry, getting ready for the Messiah to come.[69] Their focus was in the right direction, but they were missing out on the benefits of Christ's death, resurrection, ascension and the giving of the Holy Spirit. Paul was determined that every church he established should be a New Covenant church, founded on the reconciling work of the cross and sharing in the resurrection life of Jesus. So he taught them, baptised them in Jesus' name and saw each of them filled with the Holy Spirit.[70]

Thanks to Paul, the Ephesian church was as well-endowed as the church in Jerusalem at Pentecost. Whatever the level of love for God and for one another they had before they met Paul, that level would have risen considerably once they experienced the infilling of the Holy Spirit. It was this Holy Spirit-inspired love that they later left and it was probably not until they were back on track that they realised what a massive loss it had been.

I think we can assume that when the church at Ephesus left its first love, all of its major relationships were affected. God's love towards them would have remained unconditional, but the love they gave him in return would have dropped to the level of affection. The same would be true for relationships within the church. When unconditional love characterises our church relationships, even the most unlikely combinations have a way of working well. There may be some bluntness and outspokenness but the substrate of our relationships will be strong enough to take it. Unconditional love flows all the time that our relationship with God is right. It enables us to love one another with our eyes wide open.

Once the unconditional love has gone, the basis of our relationships becomes affection, which is far more conditional and prone to pettiness

69. Acts 19:1-4
70. Acts 19:5-7.

and sentimental blindness. When church relationships operate selectively, we divide people into those we like a lot and those we don't like much at all, and our likes become the basis of our relationships. When we reach beyond the church, surprisingly that pickiness can change. Faced with the warm glow of self-congratulation that spreads over us when we are doing good, we somehow find that we can stretch our affection beyond our likes and dislikes and collect some external congratulations in the process.

In leaving its first love, the Ephesian church would not have stopped reaching out to those around it. Affection works well in a needy world where even the most basic form of love is in short supply. A church operating in affection can, to some extent, fulfil the command to 'love your neighbour as yourself'.[71] It simply exchanges unconditional love for affection. But it will struggle when told to 'love the Lord your God with all your heart and with all your soul and with all your mind and with all your strength',[72] and it will not get any easier when faced with Jesus' command to 'love one another. As I have loved you ...'[73] These require unconditional love. Kindness alone will not work.

Unconditional love has to be the basis of unity – our oneness with God, our oneness with our fellow Christians and our oneness with other churches. The instruction given to all seven churches in Revelation to 'hear what the Spirit says to the churches' could, for some of them, have been a corrective and a first step to recovery.[74] A church that has settled for affection instead of unconditional love will almost certainly have problems with at least some of its inter-church relationships. Affectionate love will be far too sentimentally selective to cope. It will lack a substrate of strength, and repeatedly prove to be disappointingly short on robustness.

---

71. Mark 12:31.
72. Mark 12:30.
73. John 13:34.
74. Revelation 2:7,11,17,29; 3:6,13,22.

It is possible that the church in Ephesus, if it had stayed in its 'fallen' state, would have been too superficial and selective to actually hear what the Spirit was saying to the other six churches. It may have been moved to hear what was being said about Smyrna's suffering,[75] but have had little concern about Laodicea's lukewarmness.[76] It could have shrugged off the theological compromises at Pergamum,[77] and been totally indifferent about the opportunities promised to Philadelphia.[78] Unfortunately, having no more than a passing interest and listening to the words without hearing the depth of the needs can be characteristic of an affection-only type of love.

Some churches today have a concept of discipleship that implies we can become disciples simply by showing love. The thinking is that Jesus will happily claim as his own everyone who is especially loving and that any kind of love will do, be it *phileo* or *agape*. This is not right. Jesus intentionally used *agape* when telling us to love one another, because of the cost involved in receiving *agape* love. He made absolutely sure that his call to discipleship was about so much more than just being loving. It was a call to follow him come what may, and to do so among a group of people we might feel we could never fit in with.

It is possible that when we come to the words of the seven Revelation church leaders, we will hear echoing through them the indignation of John. They would know from their times with him that he would have been more than dismayed to hear that the radical call he and his brother heard from Jesus to 'follow me, and I will make you …'[79] could be diluted to just 'love everyone and I'll call you mine'.

---

75 Revelation 2:9-11.

76. Revelation 3:14-16.

77. Revelation 2:14-15.

78. Revelation 3:8.

79. Matthew 4:19; Mark 1:17, ESV.

John liked to state that we, as Christians, 'know that we have passed from death to life, because we love each other'.[80] We can see if we add to this statement the words of Jesus, 'everyone will know that you are my disciples, if you love one another',[81] that the *agape* love spoken of is intended to be the proof of discipleship rather than the route to discipleship. Confusion about this is hindering many churches today. The true route to discipleship is to commit to Jesus in repentance and faith and then allow him to reshape us. The love that God pours into our hearts on the day we wholeheartedly commit to him is the proof that we have signed up. Without that unconditional love there can be no real following or shaping. It would be like asking a sculptor to carve rock that no tool can crack or to mould clay that is too unyielding to shape. God works with living disciples and it is the Holy Spirit that brings God's love into our lives so that he can mould us and make us.

Let's see what the leaders of the seven Revelation churches would write to our stereotypical Conciliatory Church today.

---

80. 1 John 3:14.
81. John 13:35.

To the Conciliatory Church

[Try reading this aloud in the way the church leaders in Revelation would have read out their letters.]

Greetings from your fellow churches that have gone before you, and, after responding to the correction and encouragement of the risen Jesus, have worked together to demonstrate his love.

We commend you for your desire to show love to all, and thank you for the example you set in seeking to be one with society. We respect you for your non-confrontational style and your commitment to the marginalised.

We know that you seek to show no favouritism and we have seen how Jesus from the very beginning chose people to follow him who were very different from each other. He held them together with his love, joy and grace, looking forward to the day when his reconciling death and life-giving resurrection would enable them to receive a new level of love and unity through the coming of the Holy Spirit.

It is this new level of love, *agape* love, that we would urge you to make your own. It is this love, which God alone can give through his Holy Spirit, that marks us out as being disciples of Jesus. We know too that there is a lesser love that is more selective and less robust and it is a love that the world already knows in measure. We urge you to put being reconciled to God high on your agenda so that you can always operate in God's unconditional love, just as the Church did a few decades before us at the very beginning.

In order to know this love, each church member will have to find again the kind of relationship with God that all in the early Church knew at the outset. This will transform their lives and enable you to implement effective discipleship, which without such a relationship we all know to be impossible.

Going forward, do not be put off by those churches around you that you may consider to be unhelpfully challenging. *Agape* love brings a greater sense of bonding and you should find that inter-church relationships are no longer a delicate exercise of applying polite graciousness across a wide gulf.

In living out this love we can see you being a church that pioneers non-selective and non-sentimental relationships in a way that benefits all.

Challenge:

Write two ways in which you would proactively respond to such a letter if you were a member of a church like this.

1.

2.

3. Logistical Challenges

Although we paused our early Church narrative as Jesus prayed at the Kidron Valley before crossing over to his arrest in Gethsemane, we did move on a little as we prepared to write to the Conciliatory Church. We shared part of the post-resurrection conversation Jesus had with Peter so that we could make the point that there is an unconditional love that we can know through the Holy Spirit, going beyond the affectionate love that we can know naturally.

At the time Peter talked to Jesus, he had yet to experience the coming of the Holy Spirit, but by then Jesus had already done everything to prepare the way for the Holy Spirit to come. For centuries the separation between humanity and God had been symbolised by a thick curtain in the temple, cutting off the way into the Holy of Holies. When Jesus died, that curtain was ripped from top to bottom, indicating that, from that moment on, people were free to step into the presence of God.[82] More than that, it would be possible for the presence of God to come into people's lives. The ripping of the curtain was proof positive that the New Covenant had been established by the breaking of Jesus' body and the pouring out of his blood. His return to heaven and the sending of the Holy Spirit made it possible for the fullness of the New Covenant to be established in people's lives.

What Jesus accomplished on the cross, in terms of reconciling humanity with God, and breaking down the barriers that people erect between themselves, is absolutely fundamental to the early Church narrative.[83] It is the central point on which everything pivots. There is no Christianity without the cross, and without the preaching of the cross, and the acceptance of what it achieved, there can be no receiving of the Holy Spirit. The disciples had time to think all this through after Jesus

---

82. Matthew 27:51.
83. Ephesians 2:14-18; 2 Corinthians 5:18-21.

had ascended. He had told them to wait, and they did wait, and they waited well. They prayed and drew on their knowledge of the Scriptures. They wanted to know and show the unity Jesus had prayed for.[84] We now join them on the day before the Pentecost feast.

In their desire to be ready, they are still doing all they can to be right before God. Not knowing how long they will have to wait, they watch Jerusalem fill with visitors. It is seven weeks since the crowds had last gathered, and the people on the streets look remarkably like the ones that had shouted 'crucify' and had mocked Jesus as he dragged his cross to the crucifixion site. They want to tell the swelling crowds that Jesus is alive, and that they have seen him. They want to say that his death has not been in vain, that it is central to God's plan of redemption. But they know it will take a boldness they have yet to possess. It has been ten days since he ascended and tomorrow is the great day of the feast. Perhaps there could be some significance in that. All 120 of them settle down for the night, wondering how much they should engage in the rituals of the day ahead. They sleep fitfully and on waking, slowly enter into their daily routine. Among other things, they have been praying the prayer that Jesus taught them, reflecting on it line by line. The words 'your kingdom come'[85] seem to have grown in significance during the days they have spent together so far. 'Suddenly ...' (and here we can borrow Luke's dramatic description):

... a sound like the blowing of a violent wind came from heaven and filled the house where they were sitting. They saw what seemed to be tongues of fire that separated and came to rest on each of them. All of them were filled with the Holy Spirit and began to speak in other tongues [languages] as the Spirit enabled them.[86]

84. Acts 1:4-26.
85. Matthew 6:10.
86. Acts 2:1-4.

As they praise God in languages they do not know with a liberty that goes beyond their words, they are unaware that the sound of the wind has brought everyone from the city out of their houses into the public square. There are now thousands outside the building where they, the 120, have been waiting for the past ten days. In their excitement they hustle down the steps onto the street, still praising God and finding themselves caught up in a vast crowd that is at a loss to know what to make of them. Everyone can tell that they are speaking about the wonders God has done because they can each hear them in the languages of the nations they have come from, but beyond thinking they must be drunk, it is hard to know whatever has happened to them.[87]

Then Peter stands up and speaks in a language that is common to most, if not all.[88] He begins by quoting words from the prophet Joel about God pouring out his Spirit in the last days. As he speaks, the eleven others (Judas having been replaced by Matthias) listen and watch.[89] We can guess that some of them are wondering whatever might happen next. There have been some bold prayers prayed in the upper room over the last ten days. Their Jewish heritage had them linking Pentecost with the giving of the law, when 3,000 had tragically died.[90] Some of them had been praying for a very different 3,000 response to mark the establishing of the New Covenant, but they had no idea where such a crowd would come from or how they could possibly gather it. Now Peter was preaching to many more than 3,000, all sorts of thoughts must have been running through their minds. 'What if Peter tells them that if they repent and believe they'll experience exactly what we are experiencing? How are we going to handle the response?'

In moments such as these there is little that anyone can do other than leave things to God and be prepared to think on one's feet. Within

---

87. Acts 2:5-13.
88. Acts 21:40; 22:2.
89. Acts 2:14.
90. Exodus 32:15-28.

minutes Peter is finishing his brilliant scriptural explanation that Jesus' death, resurrection, ascension and pouring out of the Holy Spirit are all part of God's plan.[91] Suddenly he is making his appeal. True to expectations he is telling the thousands that have gathered that 'everyone who calls on the name of the LORD will be saved.'[92] What is more, while he is driving the point home with all the enthusiasm he can muster, it is obvious that God's Spirit is already working in the crowd. Peter is not offering a costless salvation. He is telling them that they have to repent and demonstrate their commitment by being baptised. He seems to be expecting a massive response, regardless of the consequences.[93]

People are already beginning to pray openly and earnestly, taking Peter's words literally. Some are already heading to the Pool of Siloam and the Pool of Bethesda. Knowing how John the Baptist baptised in the river Jordan, they are making for the two possible baptism sites in the city. A few hundred may have been manageable but they are bustling off together in their droves, all very sincere and very determined. The eleven who have been standing alongside Peter have no option but to mobilise the rest of the 120 and head off after the crowds. If they had had a minute to think about it, they would have realised that they are actually nowhere near as anxious as they might have expected. They want to support everyone in their decision, and they calmly group people together ready to step into the water. Everything is done as promptly and respectfully as emotions will allow.[94]

Once they start baptising, the excitement only increases. Those being baptised discover Peter's words to be true. No sooner have they been baptised than they know the presence of God's Spirit in and on their lives. Those who had been in the upper room encourage them reassuringly. None of it is particularly formal, but all of it is very joyful.

---

91. Acts 2:14-36.
92. Joel 2:32.
93. Acts 2:36-40.
94. Acts 2:41.

Some of those who have been baptised embrace each other, and some embrace those who have baptised them. Others find space just to stand in silent awe and wonder. Such is the measure of unity.

We can imagine how the day concludes. The crowds who have been watching gradually ebb away and eventually only those who have been baptised are left. They are reluctant to go home as they are enjoying their shared experience, appreciating each other's company and support. Gradually the word spreads: 'Let's meet again tomorrow morning – nine o'clock in Solomon's Porch. And let's invite the Twelve who were closest to Jesus to come to the temple to tell us all they learned.'

The following morning 3,000 gather, all eager to hear from the Twelve who, thanks to some hasty overnight planning, are somewhat set for the task. They will have weighed their options. They can divide the crowd into twelve groups of 200 and 300, or simply take it in turns to talk to everyone at once, valuing each other's support as they do so. We will imagine they start with everyone together and move to smaller groups as the weeks go by. They probably expect the numbers to go down as the visitors return to their home countries, but nearly everyone stays and the numbers increase as others come to join them. From day one the central teaching sessions in Solomon's Porch are interspersed with prayer, often informal in smaller groups, and the relationship-building continues in people's homes. Once they have been taught the significance of the bread and wine, they want to share that reverently when they meet in their houses.[95]

It is possible that by now all of us who are reading this are longing to become organisers. After all, the last 2,000 years have taught us how to 'do church', but we have to face the reality that spontaneous new movements are not easily contained. New problems keep demanding attention. With so many visitors staying on in Jerusalem, there were bigger, practical issues to deal with than simply organising meetings

---

95. Acts 2:42-43,46; 5:12.

that everyone seemed capable of organising among themselves. Some people would have been looking for longer-term accommodation. Many who had been baptised on the day of Pentecost had only planned to be in Jerusalem for a week, and are now thinking of staying indefinitely. Not everyone is earning, so some are unable to pay their way. There is an urgent need to raise funds. Everyone is sharing what they have, but having to house and feed so many is difficult. Some begin selling properties and bringing money to the Twelve.[96]

A food distribution programme has to be set up for the most vulnerable. This is not without its challenges. Jewish society is divided culturally into those who have embraced Greek customs and those who have shunned them. The new movement has been embracing people from all backgrounds without insisting that people conform to one cultural norm rather than the other. From the start everyone's view is that the differences will strengthen the unity and add to the excitement of all being one. There is a moment, though, when this comes under threat. A group of widows from a Greek cultural background somehow get missed out in the daily food distribution. Some want the Twelve to exercise stronger leadership but the Twelve themselves want to concentrate on their daily teaching schedule and on praying for God's guidance. Wisely they decide to involve everyone in finding a solution.[97]

The Twelve recognise that this has been a people's movement from the outset and changing that now would increase the tension. They know they are not the only ones with enough discernment to find the right people to solve the problem. They set the guidelines, define the responsibilities and agree to endorse the appointments publicly, but the selection needs to satisfy everybody. Appointing seven recognised assistants proves to be a big step forward.[98]

---

96. Acts 2:44-45.
97. Acts 6:1-4.
98. Acts 6:5-7.

Some of us may at last be sensing a growing feeling of relief. Organisation is on its way! But we should not conclude that there was no discipline before the Church made these appointments. In fact, there was a moment when God intervened to hasten two people into his presence to face his judgement. Painful though it was, it not only brought a reality check to the Church but also showed how much God was watching over the new movement to guard it against compromise. In his Sermon on the Mount, Jesus had said 'broad is the road that leads to destruction … But … narrow [is] the road that leads to life'.[99] This stands as a reminder that, welcoming though Jesus is, there are entry conditions for his kingdom. Those who are puffed up with their own self-importance or absorbed in their own self-interests are never going to make it down the narrow road that leads to the privilege of participating in his resurrection life.

The radical nature of the early Church was both an attraction and a deterrent. Finding life was attractive, but entering into it through brokenness and humility was costly. Of course it was great to be at the centre of a loving community, but that community only held together because no one thought of themselves more highly than they should.[100] In such an environment, arrogance and self-interest will stand out in sharp contrast. So let us backtrack for a moment to when properties were being sold, and pick up on the reality of early Church discipline.

Ananias and Sapphira have sold a property, partly for their own gain but also to give towards the needs of the church. Sadly, they see it as an opportunity to make a name for themselves and begin claiming that they are giving the total proceeds from the sale. They seem oblivious to the fact that they are lying in the face of the Holy Spirit, until Ananias walks into church and drops dead as Peter is exposing their deception. Three hours later when Sapphira arrives, Peter gives her an opportunity to set

99. Matthew 7:13-14.
100. Romans 12:3.

the record straight by asking her the market price of the house. When she lies, Peter, who by now has realised what God is doing, tells her that the men who are just returning from burying her husband will be carrying her out too. The two are buried together and the church moves on, much chastened and even more determined to walk in humility and truthfulness.[101]

These were exceptional days, but humility and truthfulness still need to be hallmarks of the Church today, no matter how much more organised we are and how much more docile we may have become. Low-risk Church may suit us well, but we cannot afford to opt for stagnation in preference to momentum. It is good to know that days of multiplication do not always have to be accompanied by painful subtractions, but slowing down growth will carry its own risks.

Let's now take a moment to reflect on some key points that we can take forward:

- The disciples had witnessed remarkable things in the death and resurrection of Jesus and yet when he ascended, he told them to wait. What do you think they were doing as they waited and why?
- When the Holy Spirit came, those gathered in the street would not have seen the fire but would have heard the wind and the works of God being proclaimed in multiple languages. Is there anything else they might have noticed about the 120 who had been in the upper room?
- The vast response from among the crowd at Pentecost was something the apostles may have prayed for but could hardly have prepared for. How did they cope on the day?

---

101. Acts 5:1-11.

- The subsequent enthusiasm of those who responded was also remarkable, but not without its problems. What practical steps did the Twelve take to deal with these problems going forward?
- Did the enthusiasm wane or grow?

4. Letter to the Conforming Church

As we take a break in our narrative to write to a Conforming Church, it is fair to ask, 'Why this church now?' The simple answer is that a Conforming Church is one that had great momentum to start with but now operates at a pace more in line with others. Having seen the momentum that existed in the early days in Jerusalem, we are at a good point to consider, with the leaders of the Revelation churches, the pressures that can lead to a slowing down. To do this we have to discard the idea that a loss of momentum is inevitable. It is far too simplistic to say that it just happens through the passage of time.

As we return to our imaginary town we find Glad Tidings Assembly, meeting in what was built as a mission hall in the mid-nineteenth century. It is quite a barn of a place, with Bible texts painted in scrolls on the walls and it is possible to see where the pews were originally screwed to the floor. They were replaced by wooden chairs in the 1920s when the building was last refurbished and the bulky finned radiators were installed. It is not as dowdy as it sounds, as the place is kept cleaned and painted by some of its faithful members, and there are potted plants on the windowsills. The congregation is not as small as one might expect for a building with such a long history. Although the name was changed to Glad Tidings Assembly a mere 100 years ago, some family roots go back much further, and many families have stayed faithful, travelling in from a wide area as jobs have taken them further and further afield.

The Assembly has recently welcomed a young pastor who seems to be going down well with some in their teens, a few of whom are the great-great-grandchildren of some of the original members, and labelled by their parents as 'fifth generation assembly members'. Despite such labelling, the other churches in town are almost more proud of the Assembly's history than its members are. This, though, is really a case of historical distance adding enchantment to how the Assembly is viewed, since as recently as the 1920s the Assembly was held firmly at a distance by the other churches, all of which found its evangelistic fervour hard to handle.

Much has been done by the Assembly to calm down its image since then. Its preaching is no longer so passionate and its presence in the public square has become far less rowdy since the crowds stopped gathering. Its annual conference, still a feature of Assembly life, is no longer marked by a victory parade. Gone are the days when enthusiastic members marched out from the mission hall led by the combined bands of the Boys' Brigade and Girls' Guildry with several hundred Sunday school children following behind. From time to time the members will still have a stall in the market square but it is more likely to sell cakes with 'Jesus loves you' written in the icing than to distribute tracts challenging the residents to consider their eternal destiny.

There is a nostalgia for the old days mixed in with the desire to fit in and be relevant, but the new young minister seems to be wracking his brains as to how best to harness such a mixture, not only for the present but also for the future.

What do we say to a church like Glad Tidings that clearly has been caught up in what seems to have been some widespread movement in the past? Well, we can start by acknowledging that changes within society can be a big issue for many churches, and a Conforming Church that once stepped out boldly ahead of the pack may feel it more than most, especially if at the outset it deliberately adopted patterns and practices of the day in order to gain popular appeal. However, it could be argued that those who were gifted enough to run a popular movement in one generation should be gifted enough to see their successors run an equally popular movement in another.

That said, the concept of popularity deserves closer attention. Movements are rarely popular simply because they adopt current fashions and styles. Those who are drawn in on that basis often have little staying power. People gather when they see a need being met that they feel intensely, or know that something they hold to strongly is being consistently prioritised. When these are the attraction, popularity is not the be all and end all. If it comes, it comes coincidentally from the movement's principles, not because the seeking of popularity has become the movement's principal thing.

In fact, the pursuit of popularity could be a turn-off for many as it would undermine any hope of the movement being taken seriously as a stand against the trends of the day. Loss of appeal is more likely to come from a dilution of founding principles than from a failure to keep up with the vagaries of society, whether they be vagaries of style or of thought. And of the two, trying to keep up with society's changes in thought could be more costly in terms of appeal than trying to keep up with changes in style. It is changes in thought that lead to changes in principles and an undermining of passion.

My observation is that it is not so much a desire to fit in with society that has caused some of our great Christian movements birthed in recent centuries to lose their momentum. It is true that some have worked harder than they need have done (and maybe even should have done) to keep up with fashion in style and thought but, even so, it is more often pressure from within the wider Church that slows their pace. Such pressure can be subtle as well as almost irresistible. It can come in the form of an expectation to comply with norms, or as talk about all moving forward as one, which sounds alluring but ignores the fact that eventually everything will move at the speed (if that is the right word) of the slowest. It is a pressure that has to be resisted, but as it often comes wrapped in flattering words and patronising phrases, it can be hard to spot. It is as if the strength of its grip remains hidden within a velvet glove.

Not every movement succumbs to such constraints but many do and the Church is the poorer for it. Sadly, the movements that yield to this pressure from other churches do not notice how much in yielding they are being further undervalued, so the process goes on unchecked. Movements that once flourished begin to make endless internal realignments until they are finally fully domesticated and have lost their key distinctives. They can keep some of their trappings, and may find themselves being admired for some trivialities they themselves find quite outdated, but the Church, unlike the wider world, is not troubled about being up-to-date, and seems even less troubled about domesticating the energy out of a once vibrant movement.

We are of course talking stereotypically, but in these cases where much mutual politeness abounds, questions still have to be asked about a possible aversion to difference. There is a view, which seems to lie beneath the surface for many, that success in one quarter will lead to an undermining of commitment in another. There may be a hint of jealousy here, but it is amazing how much some people fear shifts in church loyalties, even when people are still staying committed to Christ, or becoming even more committed to him.

We all know that none of us should put loyalty to our church above our loyalty to Christ, but these things happen when we lose sight of the oneness that Christ has given us. If we think everyone in town should belong to 'us', we will end up striving for a monolithic kind of unity that God never intended us to have. He is the God of unity, not uniformity. Even creation teaches us that variety and diversity are his specialities. There really is little value in the static unity that some seem to yearn for, wanting everything to stay the same or become the same. God knows the end from the beginning, but surely it is not lost on us that he always appears to be doing new things.[102]

We have said that the New Covenant itself was God's plan from the beginning, but as the first-century Church rejoiced in it, many around them wanted to cling to the Law of Moses, putting God's interim

---

102. Isaiah 43:18-19.

arrangement ahead of his original intention. One of the joys of the New Covenant is that it will never grow old. It is God's ultimate covenant and will never be bettered in terms of what it brings to humanity. We need to understand Peter's words at Pentecost rightly if we are to appreciate how the New Covenant retains its newness from generation to generation. He declared, 'The promise is for you and your children and for all who are far off – for all whom the Lord our God will call.'[103] Why should we complain if we find that when the Lord calls those 'who are far off', they express their joy at coming to him in ways that are different from those we have grown used to? And what if they seek to fulfil their evangelistic responsibilities with enthusiastic methods that are not like our existing ones? God is entitled to bring something fresh in every generation, and within the freshness of God's New Covenant, new expressions do not have to lead to the abandonment of previous ones.

If a new movement is right in what it is doing, there is no reason why it cannot keep doing it. The Church-world does not have to follow the world of fashion. This year's 'new' does not have to replace last year's 'new'. In the Church what is new this year can come alongside what was new last year to reinspire it and restate the uniqueness of its contribution. To change the picture, in making a cake, you do not take out a previous ingredient every time you add a new one. It is true that things do move on in society and churches have to keep pace, but history is valuable. It can offer us inspiration and well-tested strategies. Churches that were birthed as movements that captured the public's attention in the past, even if they were at odds with other churches at the time, need to tell their stories. They also need to keep demonstrating the things that proved to be their movement's strengths. Movements are not birthed to become monuments but to continue as living contributors, joining others in making room for what may come along as new later.

As we come to consider our second letter from the leaders of the seven

---

103. Acts 2:39.

Revelation churches, we can imagine them looking back and asking what caused some of their churches to slow down. The Ephesian church had once received a letter from Paul, some years before John moved into the area.[104] It may well have been circulated to the other six Aegean churches and handed on by Laodicea to the church at Colossae too.[105] As Paul wrote, the tremendous spiritual breakthrough that had occurred through his teaching in the School of Tyrannus must have been at the front of his mind.[106] He knew the strength of the Ephesian believers' calling. It had sustained them through those early days when the gospel response in Ephesus was so strong that it eventually led to a riot in the amphitheatre.[107] He was not going to see the hope of that calling fade away. In his letter he wrote, 'I pray that the eyes of your heart may be enlightened in order that you may know the hope to which he has called you'.[108] God's calling really counts. It counted when Paul wrote his letter, and it still counted a few decades later when John recorded the letter from Jesus exhorting the Ephesian believers to return to their first love.

We can also see the leaders weighing the words Jesus gave John for the church at Philadelphia: 'I have placed before you an open door that no one can shut.'[109] They would have known that when God opened a door for the church in Philadelphia, he did not close doors he had previously opened or shut doors he had opened for others. They would also have been relieved to realise they had not inadvertently closed Philadelphia's door by persuading its members to adopt some of their more complacent approaches. Until Jesus spoke, they may not even have been aware of the opportunities the Philadelphians were enjoying, or of the pressures that were bringing them near to the end of their strength.

---

104. Paul's letter to the Ephesians.
105. Colossians 4:16.
106. Acts 19:8-10.
107. Acts 19:17-41.
108. Ephesians1:18.
109. Revelation 3:8.

With hindsight, the importance of keeping an 'open door confidence' can seem blazingly obvious. Losing it would not only have been costly for Philadelphia, but also for their local community, for the churches across the region and for the generations to come. If the six other churches had known sooner what God was doing with the church in Philadelphia, they may have been inspired to reorder themselves even before their corrective letters arrived. We need exemplary churches. It is good to believe, though, that when Jesus shook them up with his letters, they all became churches worth following.

With this in mind, let's consider a letter from the leaders of the Revelation churches. Hopefully it will inspire those churches that have emerged from the many church movements birthed over the last twenty centuries. We still need them to be inspirational today.

To the Conforming Church

[Try reading this aloud in the way the church leaders in Revelation would have read out their letters.]

Greetings from your fellow churches that have gone before you and came to value the open door that God longs to set before us all.

We appreciate your desire to move forward with others and commend you for putting in place structures that have helped you continue beyond your early years. We urge you not to lose sight of your beginnings. We take heart from the fact that God specialises in keeping doors open and we are confident that the unique calling that God raised you up to fulfil is still needed. It is vital that you do not lay that calling aside simply to comply with the styles and priorities of others.

We urge you to rekindle the fervour of your early days and to make sure you are still known for those early strengths. Never be cowered by those whose formation preceded yours or allow yourself to be intimidated by those who have come since. Share your founding passion for the benefit of all. Remember that in dialling down in order to comply, you could be masking the full diversity of God's creativity.

But do not live in the past. The battles you won in your early days were not won by relying on your previous reputation. They were won because you had no reputation to protect and little bureaucracy to preoccupy you. Your early lack of organisational strength may have helped you to be a mobile and flexible force in God's hands, able to respond swiftly to bring the good news of salvation into the lives of society's most needy. That surely remains the priority around which to mobilise your people today and we urge you still to have mobilisation as your watchword. The battle is not new and the weapons of prayer, passion and proclamation that worked for you in the past do not need replacing. We would encourage you to take the lead on such things and once again inspire others.

There was a time when the question of relevance concerned us too as we saw trends and changes within society. We stand with you in prioritising meeting needs ahead of following shifting patterns. We know that for every individual who has a need met, there is a personal relevance that surpasses any relevance which might come from a trend followed.

Above all, be bold and encourage that boldness to be evident in the lives of everyone who aligns with you. We are not urging you to put the clock back. That is not what turning around meant for us, far from it. We are sure it is the world you are in right now that needs the energy of your early impact.

Challenge:

Write two ways in which you would proactively respond to such a letter if you were a member of a church like this.

1.

2.

5. Countering Containment

At its beginning the whole Church was very much contained within Jerusalem. Those following the Way (as the Church was initially known) wanted to stay there as long as possible so they could learn from the Twelve.[110] Gradually some moved back to their home areas to establish communities of believers. Groups formed around Judea in places such as Lydda and Joppa,[111] and while the spread stayed relatively local, the Jerusalem link was able to stay strong, especially around feast times. Things began to change with the wider mobilisation that followed the appointment of the seven.[112] We pick up the story as Philip considers going to Samaria and Stephen becomes embroiled with a synagogue in Jerusalem that served the Jews from Cyrene and Alexandria as well as some from the Roman provinces of Asia and Cilicia. Both Stephen and Philip face difficult assignments.

The Synagogue of the Freedmen, as it is called, is angry. Stephen has spoken out boldly around Jerusalem about God's message of salvation through Jesus. There have been some impressive miracles but it is his ability to win arguments that is proving most annoying. So the synagogue members start stirring up the crowd by saying Stephen is teaching against Moses and claiming that Jesus will destroy the law and the temple. Their accusations result in him being dragged before the Sanhedrin, the Jews' governing council. He has to defend himself before the high priest and, in line with convention, recites the nation's story from Abraham to the present.[113]

It is when his account reaches the present day that anger suddenly erupts in the council chamber. He accuses the Sanhedrin directly,

---

110. Acts 2:42-47.
111. Acts 9:32,36.
112. Acts 6:1-7.
113. Acts 6:8 – 7:3.

pointing out quite bluntly that they are limiting God by their devotion to the temple and that they have a long history of persecuting God's prophets. He tells them that their predecessors persecuted those who predicted the Messiah and now they have betrayed and murdered the Messiah himself.[114] As the temperature rises, it is as if Stephen knows what they are about to do. He looks up to heaven and says he sees Jesus standing at the right hand of God as if waiting to receive him. Immediately they begin jostling him out through the streets and beyond the city walls. They give their coats to a young man called Saul, and stone Stephen, killing him as he asks Jesus to forgive them and receive him.[115]

Although the radiance of an open heaven may have been reflected in Stephen's face, it is a dark day for the Church. The young man who looked after the coats plans to make Stephen the first martyr of many. He begins a campaign to totally stamp out the Way.[116] Those who have been planning to return home hastily pack and leave, spreading far and wide. Ironically, the persecution is already causing the Church to grow as people share the good news of Jesus as they travel.[117] Bravely the Twelve stay on in Jerusalem to rebuild the local church. All around them the onslaught of house-to-house searches, imprisonments and even deaths seems relentless.[118]

Philip endures the barrage along with everyone else, but he still has his heart fixed on preaching to the Samaritans. Samaria lies between Judea and Galilee and, although Jesus saw a breakthrough there, it is still regarded as a no-go zone by many Jews. There is widespread uneasiness about the Samaritans' mixed heritage. On arrival, Philip holds back nothing, and his preaching is a remarkable success.[119] It is not long

---

114. Acts 7:47-53.
115. Acts 7:53-60.
116. Acts 8:1-3.
117. Acts 8:4
118. Acts 26:10.
119. Acts 8:4-8.

before the news gets back to Jerusalem, and Peter and John, despite the pressures they are facing, decide to pay a visit.[120] Looking back we might see this as a desire for the Jerusalem church to stay in control. We would be wise, though, to think of the bigger picture. Given how quickly everything is expanding, it is probably more about giving one another friendly support.

Peter and John arrive to discover that Philip has seen many miracles and baptised large numbers, including Simon, a local sorcerer who has obviously been feeling outclassed. They are thrilled with what they see but, knowing the way in which those who repented and were baptised on the day of Pentecost received the Holy Spirit, they want the Samaritan church to be just as empowered as they were at the beginning. As they lay hands on the new believers and pray for them, the Samaritans receive the Holy Spirit.

On seeing this, Simon the sorcerer is blown away. This is an even bigger miracle than all those he has seen so far. He wastes no time in offering Peter and John money so he can do what he has just seen them do. Instantly his true motives are exposed and his deceptive sway over the people is broken once and for all. Before Peter and John head back to Jerusalem, they leave Simon in no doubt that it is now up to him whether or not he repents and gets right with God.[121] Philip moves on too. What God has done in Samaria fills him with confidence. His next assignment sees him involved in God's initial steps towards establishing an Ethiopian church.[122]

Holding the growing church together is clearly going to have to be more organic than organisational. Unity will have to be a continuing work of the Holy Spirit. The church in Jerusalem will always be loved and respected but it will be the Holy Spirit who will be the international

---

120. Acts 8:14.
121. Acts 8:15-24.
122. Acts 8:26-39.

unifier. All of this will require a lot of grace and the Jerusalem church has been setting a great example. As people scattered, it could so easily have demanded ongoing ties and regular feedback, but instead it was content to watch excitedly and listen for news. People were becoming 'witnesses in Jerusalem, and in all Judea and Samaria, and to the ends of the earth', just as Jesus had said.[123] The Twelve had equipped people to share sound teaching and to apply it faithfully. Philip had done this in Samaria, marking a shift to a new level. An even greater shift would now be needed to reach the ends of the earth. The lightness of touch and the relational commitment shown by Peter and John in Samaria would continue to be important.

Let's now take a moment to reflect on some key points that we can take forward:

- Initially the church in Jerusalem was the only church that existed. How did the pressure that came upon it affect its witness and its role as a future template for others?
- As the Jerusalem church was scattered by persecution and new churches were formed, what kind of links were established between the Jerusalem church and these developing churches?
- Is there evidence of an early church-planting strategy other than moving on from persecution? If so, how would you define such a strategy?
- As church-planting increased, how do you think the new churches took account of the culture of the cities in which they were established?
- With the Jerusalem church being such a strong model, how much variation do you think was possible, or was conformity the order of the day?

---

123. Acts 1:8.

6. Letter to the Comprehensive Church

As we think about the letter that might be sent to a Comprehensive Church, we have the model of the Jerusalem church before us. In the beginning it had no choice other than to be a Comprehensive Church. It was the only point of provision. But that will not be the case for a Comprehensive Church today, and that is why we continued our narrative until the Jerusalem church became one among others.

When it comes to a Comprehensive Church being one among others, we need to look at Life Centre, which we will imagine has recently taken over a cinema in the town not far from Glad Tidings Assembly. No one can deny that Life Centre has grown rapidly and is making an impact on the community. It has made no effort to make the cinema look more church-like, and uses the display boards that once advertised the films to promote the church. Inside, all the cinema trappings remain, with both the main auditorium and youth auditorium having plush, tiered seating and thick-pile carpets. The cinema screens have gone, creating additional stage space and allowing a new large LED screen to be placed at the back of the stage to display the words behind the worship team and to carry the promotional videos that have replaced the notices. Further screens are to the side of the stage, and these carry close-ups of the preacher throughout their lively and entertaining sermon, during which the smoke machines that enhance the worship team's stage presence are deliberately turned off.

One cannot but be impressed with the extent of activities advertised by the mid-service promotional videos. This is definitely a church that offers something for everyone; everyone, that is, who may have a serious interest in living the Christian life. Even the children who meet in the youth auditorium at the same time as the main service are treated to ninety minutes of full-on stage-presented songs and Bible stories, with excellent communicators holding them enthralled.

Everything about Life Centre speaks of professionalism. Newcomers are made welcome and showered with publicity brochures and gifts. Every effort is made to maintain contact, and the staff team are very efficient at staffing the phones, texting messages and using social media. It is a church with a youthful feel but certainly not exclusively attended by young people. Few people who attend other local churches have visited Life Centre, but there is a fear among some local leaders that some people they would like to see attend their churches have already made their home at the cinema.

The evangelistic passion of a twenty-first century Comprehensive Church would be hard to miss. Its keenness to make the good news of the gospel accessible to everyone – children, youth, young adults, singles, marrieds, parents, 'empty nesters' and the elderly – will be clearly seen by all. Being an attractional church, it will be working hard to demonstrate its competence in every aspect of its delivery, from the way its services and events are prepared and presented to the way its facilities are constantly upgraded and consistently maintained.

With such commitments to excellence, a Comprehensive Church is likely to have plenty of available people and will know how to mobilise everyone to maximum effect with minimum pressure. Its members' gifts will be valued and its people will be likely to volunteer without complaining of being overloaded. Regardless of whether such a church is relatively new or part of one of our historic denominations, it will have a feeling of energy and purpose that is not just dependent on denominational vision and drive. The local leaders will be trusted to assess how best to meet local needs, and will have sufficient spiritual awareness to create a discipleship programme around its regular preaching and teaching that fully engages its whole congregation.

Although a Comprehensive Church will be committed to meeting all of its members' needs, there will be no embargo on members picking up information from elsewhere. In some cases this will be a mark of the church's confidence, as it may well regard the standard of its teaching to be so high that personal online searches are more likely to be for information to enhance what is taught rather than to undermine or question it. Those who search online will soon discover that there are many churches like their own, and this will engender a sense of solidarity and security among its members. Generally, a Comprehensive Church will be well managed financially so it can support a significant number of projects at home and overseas. For many people these days it may appear to be the church of first choice.

All of this sounds very positive but if we are going to write with an already God-given unity in mind and a thought of assembling the pieces, other local churches have to be taken into account. There is often a concern that a Comprehensive Church will be so committed to attracting people that it will draw people from other churches. This fear can lead to tensions in inter-church relations, and a Comprehensive Church may well withdraw from local inter-church engagement, thinking it is kinder to avoid tension and simply relate to churches elsewhere that have a similar townwide or citywide vision. Being understood can definitely feel more reassuring.

At first glance it might look as if the seven churches in Revelation will have little to offer us here. They were spaced out around the Aegean region, so when they were told to 'hear what the Spirit says to the churches'[124] it could have been that they were actually being encouraged to relate to each other as identical citywide churches. After all, each of them would have aspired to be a Comprehensive Church for their locality when they began. John may have told them about the early days in Jerusalem, and they could have responded with stories of their early days in the School of Tyrannus with Paul. Certainly, when things began in Ephesus there was no other church nearby. The nearest was probably at Antioch in Pisidia some 225 miles to the east and at that distance

---

124. Revelation 2:7,11,17,29; 3:6,11,22.

there would have been no fear of membership drift.[125] But there is more to it than this.

Paul always sought to raise up comprehensive churches, committed to reaching every part of a town's population as well as the region beyond. Even when the other six churches in the region came into being, although not directly planted by Paul, they would all have followed a similar pattern to that of Ephesus, each seeking to serve its own distinct community. However, while the intervening distances removed any competitive threats, they did not aid accountability. And accountability is definitely something that is raised about comprehensive churches today. So let's pursue it further.

The problem over accountability seems to track back to a combination of a sense of self-sufficiency and a desire to relate to similar churches, often ones that seem to have progressed further on their journey, making distance no object. With today's technology, connectivity creates an impression of closeness that can actually be an illusion. We watch another church or preacher on a screen and feel that we know them. We visit their churches and are treated to the special guest tour and feel privileged. We see as much of them as they want us to see and they see as much, or as little, of us as we wish to reveal. These relationships can be inspiring and rewarding but in reality, offer little in terms of true accountability as no hard questions ever get asked.

How much the seven Revelation churches knew of each other's faults and challenges before Jesus exposed them, we may never know. Even if they did know, the exhortation to 'hear' rather implies that they had not been taking a great deal of notice. Of course, it would be easy for each one to argue that it had its own issues to resolve without worrying about a church forty or even 100 miles away, and given some of the problems around the seven, the temptation to stand alone must have been really strong. But Jesus obviously expected them to stand together. Two bright

---

125. Acts 13:13-52; 14:24.

lights and five flickering ones were not going to light up the region, no matter how brilliantly the two bright lights shone. Jesus made it plain that he wanted all seven lights to burn strongly and to burn together. Mutual accountability still has its place today.

If we were able to draw out the seven Revelation church leaders independently, it might be those from Thyatira who would speak out first. They had the experience of things going wrong beneath the surface of church life and would have had grounds for pointing out that a strong church can risk becoming so self-sufficient that it will not always notice if things start to go awry. Their experience with Jezebel would back this up most dramatically, and blaming the seducer while letting off those who are seduced is simply not good enough.[126] Too many church leaders, especially high-profile ones, think themselves to be seduction-proof; they fail because they have no accountability structures in place. Sometimes we have to be prepared to think the unthinkable, even though it does not fit with our inclination towards a kindness that prefers to ignore rather than confront. Bringing such topics forward to a Comprehensive Church can seem so judgemental that we will be silencing ourselves lest we be accused of jealousy even before we have fully formed our concerns. However, the unthinkable sometimes does indeed happen, and not only within a Comprehensive Church. Sadly, it is often the case that the bigger or more profiled the church is, the greater will be the fall.

Moving on from accountability, some of the other Revelation church leaders might want to make sure that a church being comprehensive does not result in a wider experience of Church life being denied to its members. That is certainly a concern for some about a Comprehensive Church today. Those in the first century who were older would have recalled how Timothy and others were released to join Paul in his

---

126. Revelation 2:19-21.

journeys.[127] They would be keen to know if similar opportunities still exist in our day. The Roman Empire gave freedom for people to move around, so work commitments and a desire to encourage others saw people travelling from church to church.[128] Church leaders back then would always have been keen to present the wider picture, knowing that failure to do so could hinder some people's ministry as well as restrict the local church's vision. They would not be preaching the kind of allegiance to their own local congregations that caused people to stay firmly fixed within its own programmes and projects.

While most churches that aspire to be a Comprehensive Church today would definitely want to avoid this kind of locked-in mentality, there are a few that demand an unreasonable and controlling level of commitment. It is true that 'a town built on a hill cannot be hidden,'[129] and a high-profile church cannot be overlooked. However, a town on a hill can have a lot hidden within, and a high-profile church can conceal much that can be missed. Transparency has to be a much-valued commodity.

With all this in mind, let's see how the seven Revelation church leaders might write their letter.

127. Acts 16:1-3; 1 Timothy 4:14; 2 Timothy 1:6.
128. Romans 16:1.
129. Matthew 5:14.

To the Comprehensive Church

[Try reading this aloud in the way the church leaders in Revelation would have read out their letters.]

Greetings from your fellow churches that have gone before you and embraced a vision of providing comprehensively for our communities.

It is a joy to hear of your enthusiasm for the gospel and your commitment to making the Word of God known. We love your focus on mobilising your whole congregation and for keeping individuals growing in their living relationship with the Lord Jesus. Your evangelistic zeal is something that excites us as, once we were all back on track, we were keen to reach out to those around us.

We encourage you, from our own experience, to think more widely than your own work and that of those churches that are similar to you. It is through engagement that your influence can be felt most positively. What we discovered regionally, you can discover locally. You have much with which you can inspire, but be sensitive to your fellow churches. Listen to what the Holy Spirit is saying to them and respect that, even while you weigh what he is saying to you. We all have different strengths and opportunities.

In particular we urge you to be watchful and to make sure that you are held to account by those you trust. We are aware that problems can affect us all and that there is a need for us to be accountable to one another. Sadly, busyness and preoccupation with our own affairs can cause problems to go unrecognised and unchecked. It is better to deal with them when they are small than wait until they have been allowed to grow and risk affecting everybody. We have had to learn that there is a place for bearing one another's burdens.

Finally, we are aware that you attract people from right across the area, and we realise that none of us can build effectively with those we would be wiser to release. We urge you to also be prepared to release people into wider areas of service. God is building his Church, which is larger and more varied than any of our churches will ever be on their own, and it is important for all of us to hold to the bigger picture.

The psalmist said, 'There is a river whose streams make glad the city of God'.[130] We realised that when our streams flowed together, our region was better watered. The streams that we as churches bring to the community may vary in size but all are relevant for securing the widest possible local transformation.

Challenge:

Write two ways in which you would proactively respond to such a letter if you were a member of a church like this.

1.

2.

---

130. Psalm 46:4.

7. Facing Complexity

We left our early Church narrative as the Church began to spread. Until the breakthrough in Samaria, the growth was occurring almost entirely among the Jews. This is not surprising as those who had come to Jerusalem at the post-ascension Pentecost feast were either Jewish by birth or had become followers of Judaism through identifying with the Jewish communities in their home cities. It was these communities that would have been reached out to first when those scattered from Jerusalem returned home.

In explaining the good news about Jesus to their fellow Jews, they would have been able to build on well-known scriptural promises that point to Jesus as the Messiah. But Jesus had told the Twelve to go and 'make disciples of all nations,'[131] and Peter had preached on the day of Pentecost that God would pour out his Spirit on all people. The Church now needed to discover how to get beyond the Jewish few to the global many. Reaching out to the Samaritans had been a first step, but even in Samaria there was some knowledge of the beliefs and practices of their near neighbours. A Gentile strategy would be required. Unexpectedly the process begins with the conversion of Saul of Tarsus, the persecutor of the Church.

When the risen Jesus confronts Saul on the road to Damascus, he knows that Saul's conscience has been troubled ever since Stephen's death. In fact, Saul's inner uneasiness may go back even before that. His immediate willingness to submit to Jesus rather proves that deep down he had been in two minds about Jesus for a long time, even while trapped in his own darkness. It is amazing that the light of God's presence, which drives out his inner darkness and obliterates his pharisaical thoughts and commitments, should leave him temporarily blinded. But being

---

131. Matthew 28:19.

free from his turmoil and pride, he is content to be led by the hand into Damascus.[132]

God has arranged for him to be prayed for and counselled in a house on Straight Street by Ananias, a local Jewish believer. Saul's eyes are opened, and he is baptised and filled with the Holy Spirit. He is told that he is being sent to the Gentiles but starts by preaching about Jesus in the synagogues of Damascus.[133] One cannot help feeling that in these early days God is not only being extremely gracious to Saul but also to the believers in Jerusalem, who have been so traumatised by him. If Jesus had met Saul immediately as he left Jerusalem, he would have been taken back into that city. It is the believers in Damascus who have the privilege of standing with him at first, giving him and others time to come to terms with the transformation.

But the believers in Damascus see Saul's restlessness. He has a commission from the risen Lord to go to the Gentiles, but questions of how God envisages Gentiles coming to faith and living as believers have yet to be settled. He knows that no one but God can advise him. He decides to go to Arabia to take time out on his own and pray.[134] How can he, who is so steeped in Judaism, reach the Gentiles who know nothing of Moses' law or the promises of Scripture? If he is going to win the Gentiles without imposing Jewish culture on them, just how much is he going to have to change?

In his solitude he comes to terms with being a Jew to the Jews and a Gentile to the Gentiles.[135] He needs to embrace a whole new mindset and to immerse himself in a different culture if God is to raise up a new style of church. In his mind's eye he can see gatherings where Jew and Gentile worship side by side as followers of the crucified and risen Lord. He will focus on the reconciling work of the cross that has opened

132. Acts 9:1-9; 2 Corinthians 5:16.
133. Acts 9:10-22.
134. Galatians 1:11-18.
135. 1 Corinthians 9:20-22.

the way for unity between God and humanity and between Jew and Gentile too.[136] He has had his ambitions within Judaism but now he has to embrace the cross and die to his self-interests. By the time he returns to Damascus he has a strategy that will undergird his calling. But his time in Damascus is drawing to a close. His preaching in the Jewish community has upset some, and they are now plotting to kill him. It is time to return to Jerusalem.[137]

Although three years have passed since he was last there,[138] his arrival is a test for the Jerusalem church. They have heard the news of his conversion and have praised God for it, but it is Barnabas who opens the way for Saul to stay with Peter. Saul is free to move around Jerusalem and makes a point of preaching to the Hellenistic Jews. Once again there are death threats against him and he takes these as a sign to head for Tarsus, his home region.[139] Here he will begin to fulfil his calling, well aware of Jesus' words that 'A prophet is not without honour except in his own town, among his relatives and in his own home'.[140] A few believers from the Jerusalem church accompany him as far as the port at Caesarea.

We have no record of what Peter made of their time together. Maybe he was beginning to think Saul could concentrate on being a Gentile to the Gentiles while he would be a Jew to the Jews. He was comfortable travelling around Judea and was soon heading off again to Lydda and Joppa.[141] But God had other plans for Peter. His preaching on repentance and faith had opened the door of God's kingdom for 3,000 Jews and Jewish converts at Pentecost. His preaching was about to be the key that would open the door for the Gentiles. We could say that Saul had the

136. Ephesians 2:13-18; Galatians 3:26-29.
137. Acts 9:23-25.
138. Galatians 1:18.
139. Acts 9:26-30; Galatians 1:19-24.
140. Mark 6:4.
141. Acts 9:32-42.

calling, and had done the homework, but Peter had the privilege.[142] No doubt the unity they had established in their short time together left no room for any disappointment or competitiveness. They each knew the other to be equally called and equally privileged and neither would have worried if Peter, having seen Gentiles in Judea come to faith, was followed by Saul seeing something similar in Cilicia. Self-interest would not be allowed to compromise God's kingdom. It is just that God often does things in ways we do not expect.

Peter is resting in Simon's home. In the past few days he has seen some remarkable miracles – the healing of a paralysed man in Lydda, then the raising of Dorcas from the dead in Joppa where he is now. He is praying on his host's roof as mealtime approaches when suddenly he has a vision. A sheet containing animals, birds and reptiles that are banned under Jewish food laws comes down in front of him and he hears a voice telling him to eat. As he protests, the same offer is made twice more. Before he fully understands what he has seen, three men call out from the gate asking for him. He knows he should go with them so after a night's rest and some explanations, they head for Caesarea.[143]

A God-fearing, Gentile centurion called Cornelius is waiting for them with his whole household. Peter feels uncomfortable, even though he knows Cornelius has specifically sent for him. He shares his vision and his embarrassment before starting to tell them about Jesus. He has hardly begun when he hears something he first witnessed with the 120 in the upper room. As those listening are filled with the Holy Spirit, they begin praising God in other languages.[144] Peter is in no doubt as to what has just happened. While he was preaching, they had had a change of heart and reached out to God in faith. He goes ahead and baptises them.[145]

---

142. Matthew 16:19.
143. Acts 10:9-23.
144. Acts 10:24-46.
145. Acts 10:47-48.

When he reports back to the Jerusalem church, he explains it by saying, 'to Gentiles God has granted repentance that leads to life'.[146] On a later occasion he talks of God having 'purified their hearts by faith'.[147] Once again the keys of repentance and faith have opened the hearts of the hearers so they can receive new life through the Holy Spirit.

Now all of this takes place while Saul is away working in Cilicia. We know little of the progress he makes in winning over the Gentiles in his eight or nine years there. Eventually he shares with the Corinthian church some of his early trials, and it makes for a challenging read. He mentions floggings, beatings and lashings.[148] Later on, when he writes to the church in Rome, he greets believers there whom he seems to know well, even though he has never visited the city.[149] Some of them may be converts from his early years.

But Cilicia is not the only place to experience an early Gentile breakthrough. After Peter's visit to Caesarea, Antioch in Syria sees a church raised up that is notable for reaching out to Jews and Greeks. News of this makes such an impact on the church in Jerusalem that Barnabas is sent to Antioch to show Jerusalem's support. He soon finds himself thinking of Saul and sets off across the Amanus Mountains to Cilicia to find him. Remembering the notoriety Saul seems to gain whenever he preaches, he soon tracks him down and brings him back to Antioch so they can work together with the church leaders there.[150]

At this point we are going to pause to consider a letter to the Curious Church. We have seen the early Church extend its reach into the Gentile world and we now need to see what lessons that might have for us today.

---

146. Acts 11:18.
147. Acts 15:9.
148. 2 Corinthians 11:23-27.
149. Romans 16:6-15.
150. Acts 11:19-26.

Let's now take a moment to reflect on some key points that we can take forward:

- Saul needed to become established in his new-found faith before fulfilling his calling to the Gentiles. How did his time in Damascus enable this to happen?
- It would seem that Saul's time away in Arabia may have had as much to do with his future as with his past. What issues might he have been wrestling with in this time alone with God?
- Before Saul headed off for the Gentile world, he revisited Jerusalem. Why was this important?
- Saul, writing later as Paul, says, 'To those under the law I became like one under the law ... To those not having the law I became like one not having the law ...'[151] How did he set about putting this into practice?

---

151. 1 Corinthians 9:20-21.

8. Letter to the Curious Church

In today's world of inter-church relations it seems that a Curious Church is the one most likely to be held up as a role model. It is a church that would like to find out more about other churches – even those that are unlike itself – and will go out of its way to make enquiries in order to establish a friendly level of mutual acknowledgement.

St Saviour's is an unlikely candidate for a Curious Church. It is a small evangelical Anglican church with a traditional approach to worship, tucked away in the backstreets of our imaginary town. It is noteworthy for the fact that its faithful but ageing congregation is augmented by a number of retired clergy from a nearby retirement home. The vicar himself is ten years off retirement, which he considers secures him enough experience to fend off the inevitable torrent of advice. He did find himself stretched, though, when a doctor from the local hospital arrived at the vicarage with a request to use the church hall every Sunday afternoon for a multicultural Christian fellowship that until recently had met in a community hall on the other side of town. For four weeks they had been of no fixed abode as the community hall had secured a preferential booking, and they had been forced to meet temporarily in a hotel conference suite. After taking a few notes, the vicar suggested that the doctor should phone him in a few days when he had had a chance to chat to the churchwardens and some members of the church council.

To be honest, knowing how reserved his people were, he was not hopeful, and something in him was quite relieved at the thought of not having to justify to the retired clergy what they would almost certainly see as a rash move, full of potential theological compromise. But things did not go entirely as expected. The churchwardens were positive and wanted the proposal to go to the church council. A week later an extraordinary meeting of the council voted it through on a slender majority, with curiosity winning out over caution. The secretary to the council began work on preparing forms and setting in place the correct procedures. The doctor was hopeful and was prepared to wait.

By now, news of what was happening had reached the retired clergy. Caution was very definitely their watchword and they asked if they could meet the doctor. The vicar was non-committal but said he would see what could be arranged. The doctor not only agreed but offered to go with the vicar to meet them at the retirement home. The conversation was not easy, as preconceptions of what a multicultural fellowship might be like were deeply entrenched and the doctor could not hide the fact that the fellowship's style of worship was about as far removed from a prayer book service as it is possible to be. It would be great to say that the caution evaporated and that the curiosity led to commitment, but that was not the case. When the new arrangements came into play, it was obvious that any link between the Sunday afternoon gatherings and Morning Prayer would be tenuous at best and take a long time to establish.

Sometimes a Curious Church has its interest sparked when, for practical reasons, it finds itself, like St Saviour's, being approached by another congregation. There are several factors that might cause this to happen. It could be, as we have already seen, that the church approaching it may want to hire its premises, or even partner in one of its projects. These days such requests can be quite common, and different churches handle them in different ways. Many will want to be gracious, but graciousness can often stop at the level of polite refusal or with a carefully drafted agreement. This is not unreasonable. Many churches will want to protect their distinctive character and guard their core beliefs. And even churches that hold their core beliefs lightly and want to project an image of generosity can still handle things quite formally. Once documentation is in place, no further questions may be asked. Against such a backdrop one can understand why a Curious Church is commended for going further than most in its generosity, but while others will assume they already know all they need to know about another church, a Curious Church will want to know more.

The question is, 'Is being curious enough?' A church that is open to sharing its buildings and projects has incredible opportunities to develop relationships with other churches beyond polite smiles and comments about the weather. However, it is often the case that the more obvious the differences are, the more superficial the conversations will remain. This lack of depth may stem from a reluctance to reveal areas of ignorance, or simply arise from our tendency to quickly start congratulating ourselves as soon as relationship-building gets underway. Paul reminded the church in Rome to 'accept one another ... just as Christ accepted you,'[152] and there is definitely a warm feeling that comes when we believe we have done this. But whenever we get such a feeling, we need to carry out a reality check. Jesus never accepted us blindly. He knew us before we came to him, and still wholeheartedly accepted us. Ever since then he has been expecting us to open up to him more and more, so that our relationship with him can go stronger and deeper. That is true acceptance and it is exactly what Paul had in mind. We need to be careful not to congratulate ourselves too prematurely and miss the richness of what we could go on to enjoy.

A Curious Church not only has to be aware of the risk of superficiality, but also be alert to some of the current trends in inter-church relations that seem to encourage this. We are stepping onto controversial ground, but it is only controversial because in writing this book we are holding to the view that we have been given a unity that we need to maintain, rather than a hope of unity that we need to strive for. When unity is seen as a given, 'acceptance' becomes the watchword. When unity is seen as a goal, 'receptivity' becomes a useful word for describing the necessary first tentative steps towards finding it. Acceptance says, 'I need to accept you as Christ has accepted me, and, because he has just as eagerly accepted

___
152. Romans 15:7.

you, we are one, regardless of our differences.' This kind of acceptance is not blind acceptance. It is an eyes-wide-open, dive-right-in, let's-keep-on-thrashing-out-our-differences kind of acceptance. It has to be strong because we cannot lightly dismiss each other, but it can also be blunt, since as we get to know each other we can offer corrections according to our convictions. It is not a static unity. In correcting each other, we can change. It is in fact a robust oneness worthy of a God who laid down his life to create it.

Now it would be great if 'receptivity' were just another way of saying 'acceptance', but acceptance is about being committed whereas receptivity is about being open to explore, and even that is not the same as being open to commit. And even being open to commit is not the same as being committed. Let me offer you two pictures from Ezekiel's vision of the valley of dry bones. The first picture is of a battlefield strewn with disconnected bones. Ezekiel is told to prophesy to the bones and he sees them come together. Suddenly there are no longer any unattached bones and every skeleton is complete and fully covered in flesh. In the second picture, which follows on from it, we see a whole army before us. It is still on the battlefield so we are not looking at rank upon rank of terracotta-like warriors lined up on a parade ground waiting for a ceremonial march-past but at regiments and contingents all in position, ready to engage. Once again Ezekiel is told to prophesy, but this time he is not going to be prophesying to the bones. He follows God's instructions and prophesies to the wind so that the army becomes alive and fit for battle. The question is simple: which picture expresses better where the Church is at today?

Judging by the cautious explorations some are undertaking, we must be raising tranches of field archaeologists ready to tiptoe around the battlefield and painstakingly test, identify and catalogue our bones in the hope of reassembling us and placing us on display. The patience involved in this is not something Ezekiel would have bothered with.

Even in phase one of his vision, with a picture of dereliction before him, he prophesied to the bones and everything came together in an instant. I believe Christ's death on the cross provided such a reconciling moment for those called to be his Church. In the second picture, everything is in place and all that is needed is to prophesy to the wind.[153] This is where my optimism takes me. The God who blew at Pentecost can blow on his Church again today.

Now let me bring a third picture, this time from the building site rather than the battlefield. God gave us unity by giving us his Spirit, and over the centuries we have built structures around that unity. There is an interlinkage between what we have built and what God has been building, and the two are so entwined that to try to demolish our own efforts might damage what he has done. If what we have built is restrictive rather than merely irrelevant, or distracting rather than simply decorative, the good news is that what God has been building is strong enough and flexible enough to contain all the life he wants us to have. Sufficient to say that our real unity will always be organic rather than organisational, and advocating the robustness of acceptance rather than the caution of receptivity should be seen in that light. We do not need to act as if what God has built needs deconstructing and rebuilding. That would indeed be daunting, and incredibly time-consuming and labour-intensive!

There is a further factor that may keep the interactions of a Curious Church unduly superficial and unnecessarily cautious. It is what some see as Paul's qualification to his exhortation to 'accept one another … just as Christ accepted you.'[154] The supposed qualification is also in his letter to the Romans and reads, 'Accept the one whose faith is weak, without quarrelling over disputable matters.'[155] Two things here

---

153. Ezekiel 37:1-10.
154. Romans 15:7.
155. Romans 14:1.

might make a Curious Church nervous: Firstly, are the people it wants to find out more about 'weak in faith'? Secondly, might they want to discuss trivial things that could result in a quarrel? Ninety-nine times out of 100 the answer will be 'no', on both counts. It is a warped sense of kindness that makes us think otherwise. Why should we consider others to be weaker in faith than we are? And why should we assume that anything they want to discuss will be so marginal that it could be classified as disputable, let alone result in a quarrel? Nonetheless, there is wisdom in observing carefully before engaging in discussion, and the more immersive those observations are, the more informed the discussions will be. To avoid superficiality, curiosity should always lead to engagement. Those who want to be bridgebuilders should first cross the river, then build the bridge back from the other side. This is what immersive observation is all about.

The Curious Church might well reflect on the fact that although the distance between Simon's home in Joppa and Cornelius' house in Caesarea was relatively small geographically, it was absolutely huge culturally. Peter bravely crossed the gap and what happened as a result permanently changed his mindset. Saul, as Paul was known at the time, was even more rigorous in his determination to make the crossover. Having taken time out to seek God in depth in Arabia, he threw himself into Gentile culture in Syria and Cilicia. He was not just thinking of dipping briefly into another world, but immersing himself for a lifetime. Whether a Curious Church models itself on Peter or Saul, it will have to step out well beyond its comfort zone if it is to have a similar life-changing experience.

With all this in mind, we need to consider the likely thoughts of our Revelation church leaders as we have them write their letter. The distinction between 'receptivity' and 'acceptance', though important for us, would not be important for them. They had the benefit of being raised on the inclusive theology of Paul, which he had developed earlier when he was still known as Saul. They would, however, know a lot about superficiality. The churches at Ephesus, Sardis and Laodicea all suffered from having allowed things to become far too shallow.[156] In putting things right they would have had to have developed insightful relationships with the other churches. These would have been far from superficial and would have to have gone way beyond mere curiosity. Painful though it was to have their faults exposed to each other, it meant they were no longer relating superficially in ignorance but wholeheartedly in genuine, unconditional love. In the end they discovered that they needed each other's support more than they feared each other's judgement.

Let's see how they might frame their letter.

---

156. Revelation 2:4; 3:1,15.

To the Curious Church

[Try reading this aloud in the way the church leaders in Revelation would have read out their letters.]

Greetings from your fellow churches that have gone before you and benefited from the corrective words of Jesus to 'hear what the Spirit is saying to the churches'.

We are keen that your interest in others will continue to grow. We see you opening up a way for others to follow. We had to reach out afresh to each other as churches, going beyond our previous curiosity and superficiality, in order to engage constructively. We can see that there is strength in relationships where nothing is hidden and Jesus certainly ensured that there was nothing hidden between us.

As you celebrate the diversity you find, we urge you to make sure you are confident about your own ground and are prepared to answer probing questions as well as to pose them. We can see that a depth of enquiry is a mark of respect, whereas superficiality can be patronising and leave us engaging sentimentally. Those you accept will want to accept you too.

Our cities differed greatly from each other and our practices differed too. We needed to be culturally aware and you will need to be too. It is a good preparation for handling greater diversity within your own congregation. Allow friendship to win over formality.

We are confident that as you press on in your quest you will be an inspiration to all and find a freedom and openness in your new relationships that speak of the unity of the Spirit.

Challenge:

Write two ways in which you would proactively respond to such a letter if you were a member of a church like this.

1.

2.

9. Withstanding Pressure

The model for a multicultural church develops well in Antioch under what, for its day, is a remarkably diverse leadership team of teachers and prophets. Saul and Barnabas take their place alongside the three original church planters,[157] and after a year are asked to travel to Jerusalem with a gift for the churches in Judea. This was prompted by a prediction of widespread famine given by the prophet Agabus. The way that the church in Antioch responds to this prediction is an excellent example of unity working spontaneously in the first-century Church. The time that Saul and Barnabas then spend in Jerusalem gives us a further example.[158]

They arrive at a moment when a fresh round of persecution is hitting the church. This time it is initiated by Herod who, as a regional leader, still has some influence under the Romans. He has executed James, the brother of John, and has Peter in prison. The church is holding prayer meetings for Peter's release, hoping for a miracle similar to that before Saul's persecution, more than fourteen years earlier.[159] Back then, the high priest and his followers held the Twelve overnight while the church was still meeting in Solomon's Colonnade, but an angel had released them.[160] The tension turns to joy when the miracle is repeated, and as the church returns to normal, pressure is further eased by the death of Herod.[161]

During all this drama, Saul is paying close attention to the Jerusalem church. He sees how effectively James, the brother of Jesus, steps into the shoes of James the brother of John, and stands alongside Peter and John continuing to provide the space and confidence that enables everyone in the church to function freely. Despite their seniority, they seem to act

---

157. Acts 11:25; 13:1.
158. Acts 11:27-30.
159. Galatians 2:1.
160. Acts 5:17-20.
161. Acts 12:1-24.

no differently within the local church than Simeon, Lucien and Manaen, the pillars back in Antioch.[162] Nonetheless, having Peter, James and John together is too good an opportunity for Saul to miss and he meets with them privately to share the approach he has developed for preaching to the Gentiles.[163]

Ironically, while the three senior Jerusalem leaders are happily accepting this, some who claim to be part of the Jerusalem church are pressurising Titus, a young Gentile believer who has travelled with Barnabas and Saul, to be circumcised. Barnabas and Saul firmly resist this with the support of the local leaders.[164] The fluid nature of local commitment in those days is seen as Barnabas and Saul take Barnabas' cousin John Mark back to Antioch with them.[165] All of this happens despite John Mark's obvious closeness to Peter and the prominence of his mother in the Jerusalem church.[166] Their home had been used by the church to pray for Peter's release.[167] There might have been no organisational tie between the churches back then but the relational ties and mutual respect were strong.

Our early Church narrative now moves back to Antioch where once again we see how first-century churches had a vision that was not centred on the growth and prestige of their own congregation but was capable of releasing people for wider ministry. As the leaders at Antioch pray, they hear God tell them to set apart Barnabas and Saul to fulfil their church-planting role.[168] The two, who are sent out with prayer and the laying on of hands, take John Mark with them and head for Cyprus where Barnabas and some in the church at Antioch have family ties.

---

162. Galatians 2:9; Acts 13:1.
163. Galatians 2:1-2,6-10
164. Galatians 2:3-5.
165. Acts 12:25.
166. 1 Peter 5:13.
167. Acts 12:12.
168. Acts 13:2-3.

The time on the island, marked by its notable meeting in the home of the proconsul that seems to be a turning point for the dynamics of their three-man team, proves to be a launching pad for ministry on the mainland. As they move on, Saul has renamed himself Paul and is taking the lead, John Mark is planning on going home, and the team has grown as Paul has gathered others around them. Paul heads for the cities of Galatia, west of those in Cilicia where he had previously preached on his own.[169]

On the mainland they start in Perga then move on to Pisidian Antioch, Iconium, Lystra and Derbe. They preach to Jews and Gentiles and are thorough in the way they set up churches. They travel back across the same ground to appoint mature and trustworthy people in each place to watch over their new fellow Christians and encourage them to contribute to church life.[170] Paul is in effect recreating the same open and facilitating approach he has seen in Jerusalem and Antioch, ensuring that each church is safe under wise and caring oversight. Once back in Syria they report on all they have seen and done.[171]

Soon, though, a problem arises. Having been back in Antioch for a short while they hear that the churches they planted in Galatia are coming under pressure from people who, like those they encountered with Titus in Jerusalem, are insisting that Gentiles need to be circumcised and to keep the Jewish law.[172] This is not entirely a surprise as similar people have been to Antioch and caused trouble over Jewish and Gentile believers eating together. They insisted that unless someone was circumcised they could not be a true believer. They came at a time when Peter was also in Antioch and Paul had to remind him how important it was to take a stand against these pressurisers.[173] The news from Galatia prompts Paul

---

169. Acts 13:4-13.
170. Acts 13:14 – 14:25.
171. Acts 14:26-28.
172. Galatians 1:6-9.
173. Acts 15:1; Galatians 2:11-21.

to write to the Galatian believers to tell them that they must take a firm stand too. He is rigorous in putting his case, and one cannot help feeling he is drawing on a lot of the thinking he did when he took time out alone from Damascus soon after he was converted.[174]

He makes his case based on the fundamental difference between the Old Covenant and New. He focuses on the equality Jews and Gentiles have in Christ, and the freedom we can all enjoy as we no longer have to live under the burden of the Law of Moses. He argues that it is Christ's sacrifice on the cross that has liberated us and that it is the empowering of the Holy Spirit that enables us to live lives pleasing to God.[175] At this point there is no need to go into the depths of Paul's reasoning but for the sake of our early Church narrative, we need to note that unity in the first-century Church included taking a strong stand against any divisiveness that ran contrary to Scripture.

It is interesting that the leaders of the church in Antioch do not let the matter rest. They have benefited from Paul's confrontation in their local situation and know the Galatians will have been strengthened by Paul's letter, but a lasting solution needs to be found for the sake of all the churches. For this to happen they need to send Paul and Barnabas, and a team, back to Jerusalem.[176]

As they get ready to go, we will prepare to consider the letter to the Concerned Church from the leaders of the Revelation churches.

Let's now take a moment to reflect on some key points that we can take forward:

- Paul took over from Barnabas as the leader of the small mission team as they moved on from Cyprus. How did this change of leadership affect their subsequent ministry on the mainland?

---

174. Galatians 1:1-17.
175. Galatians 3:1 – 6:16.
176. Acts 15:2.

- Where churches had been established, elders were put in place. What were the responsibilities of these elders and what challenges did they face when Paul and the team returned to Antioch?

- After the team's return, the leaders at Antioch became concerned about a possible Jewish/Gentile split in the Church. What would have been uppermost in their minds as they planned to prevent this?

- Paul himself took a very strong line against those of the circumcision party, arguing that their message undermined people's freedom in Christ. Should freedom in Christ be our main concern today, or are there other issues that should concern us more?

10. Letter to the Concerned Church

A Concerned Church is a church with strong convictions. These will often be about adherence to Scripture but could equally relate to concerns about social justice. Whatever the issue happens to be, it will, characteristically, result in a firm stance being taken that could lead to separation from others on a matter of principle. A Concerned Church will not hesitate to put its point of view, and will not be embarrassed at being known either for raising related issues on a number of occasions, or for presenting a major issue persistently.

No one knows much about Ebenezer Hall, and even those who meet there do not know how the property, built in the early twentieth century, was bequeathed to them. The man who built it was obviously wealthy and yet must have had a heart for reaching the poor with the gospel, as he chose to build the hall in the least privileged part of town. St Saviour's is not far away, but the members of Ebenezer Hall are only selectively engaged in the wider aspects of local church life. The two churches may be close theologically but St Saviour's was there when the hall was built, and it is as if they were almost intended to stand apart.

That is not to say the members of Ebenezer Hall are entirely inward-looking. Whereas other churches might hope to bring people into their buildings, the members of Ebenezer Hall are prepared to be out where the people are, at least physically, having their tracts on display in the market square and making sure they have bold conversationalists on hand. Taking this further, if other churches are prepared to hold a gospel campaign with a sufficiently biblically conservative speaker, they will support it, but 'sufficiently biblically conservative' is the key. Any deviation from that will meet with separation. No one could ever accuse Ebenezer Hall of compromise. The members are prepared to speak up for their views, but are equally inclined to walk away if no one seems to be listening.

They do have a genuine concern for the other churches in town and are dismayed to see any discarding of what they consider to be core biblical values. Even more concerning to them is the fact that they now see churches holding what they regard as socially liberal views with a tenacity that matches their own. And these churches are not so prepared to go it alone. Those from Ebenezer Hall are grateful that there are some evangelically minded churches in town that will want to stand and argue. For their part they are content to simply trust that their understanding of truth will win through in the end.

Far from being unfeeling, a Concerned Church (which is just as likely to be denominational as non-denominational) generally registers things deeply and holds its concerns unselfishly. It takes its stand for the good of others and does so with a desire to see God honoured. When it steps away from inter-church relationships it often does so with sadness, thinking it may be kinder to others and easier on itself if everyone goes their separate ways. When it no longer finds a warm welcome locally it usually finds a heartfelt acceptance among like-minded people further afield. All of this can be very disturbing in today's polite inter-church climate where strong opinions are often dealt with by trying to defuse them rather than engage with them. Listening to each other has to be a key.

As we keep in mind throughout this book the command of Jesus to 'hear what the Spirit says to the churches'[177] we need to note that of all our seven stereotypes it is a Concerned Church that is most likely to be misunderstood and ignored. And yet in its seemingly immovable mindset it has something significant to say to us all. Disagreeing agreeably runs the risk of creating an amiable fudge in which passions are subdued so that everything either creeps forward or stagnates. Even the beliefs held in common become simply accepted rather than boldly proclaimed. Sadly, this can deprive society of evangelistic input,

---

177. Revelation 2:7,11,17,29; 3:6,13,22.

as approaches to evangelism are among the things least likely to be agreed upon. Better to disagree passionately and to value each other's passion as part of the strength of our unity and to see it as an important contribution to our impact on society.

In our first-century narrative we have two competing concerns – the concern of those who genuinely believe that failure to keep the Law of Moses will cost people their salvation, and the concern of those who believe that forcing people to keep the law will rob them of their freedom in Christ. We should be able to see that the scriptural argument clearly favours the second position, and that is definitely where we take our stand. But things are not always that straightforward. There are issues that arise today where knowing how best to place our weight can be hard to discern. Wisdom dictates that when we draft our letter to a Concerned Church, we should avoid basing it on issues so that we can properly address attitudes, not only the attitudes shown by the Concerned Church but those shown towards it.

There is obviously a point in the history of the church at Antioch where it became a Concerned Church. All churches have concerns from time to time, but some issues bring out a high level of tenacity. We need to distinguish where the unyielding resolve is being focused, as misplaced resolve can be counterproductive. In Antioch the focus was definitely on upholding its understanding of the truth. The leaders at Antioch did not become entrenched in their views because they were spoiling for a fight, or because they enjoyed being contentious. We have to say in their favour that they had a concern for the truth that was well thought through, both practically and theoretically. Practically, they had raised a church where Jewish and Gentile believers could function side by side, and this was successful even before Paul arrived. When Paul came, he brought the reasoning he had worked out before God many years ago in the seclusion of Arabia. For Paul, his reasoning undergirded his calling, and both his reasoning and calling had been well tested over the years by those to whom he made himself accountable.

Alongside truth, pastoral care was also a strong factor for the church leaders in Antioch. Confusion had affected people's behaviour and had begun to undermine their faith. The risk of personal derailment had to be urgently addressed. The third factor for Antioch was unity, not only in terms of local church life but also globally. Some issues are just so much bigger than any one local congregation. The circumcision issue was in fact so big that it was in danger of splitting the growing Church worldwide. It had to be addressed with the future in mind.

The right place to go was Jerusalem, as the circumcision advocates were claiming the endorsement of James and the Jerusalem church. There had to be resolution at the source. James and the believers in Jerusalem needed to know what was being said in their name. Antioch's tenacity for the sake of global unity overrode any thought that it might be kinder to let matters rest in order to present a united front. They registered, as we must, that unity that is just a front is not really unity at all. But the clarity of Antioch's concern for both truth and unity, together with its depth of pastoral understanding, would have contributed to Jerusalem's willingness to take things forward. An agreement to meet was readily forthcoming. Antioch, a Concerned Church with a justifiable tenacity, could be confident that it was going to be well received and respectfully heard.

So, what kind of letter might our Revelation church leaders write to bring about such a positive encounter with a Concerned Church today? There certainly will need to be some encouragement to commit to truth and pastoral care, but it would seem that a commitment to unity will have to be a priority to guarantee the desired engagement. If unity is seen as a truth to hold onto rather than a goal to aspire to, a lot of ground will already have been gained.

It was a commitment to unity that drove Paul to question whether the circumcision advocates were true believers.[178] Looking back now, labelling them in such a way may seem like a piece of pettiness within a partisan debate, but preserving unity is not about being kind to each other. The unity we have been given is far too valuable to compromise. If people have come into the church in unrepentance and unbelief to undermine its core principles, it is not unreasonable to point this out. It may seem overly judgemental but half-hearted reproofs are unlikely to produce a lasting resolution. Progress is made when the strongest advocates sit down together on a 'concessions without compromise' basis. Even if convictions leave no room for resolution, both parties will be confident that they have been heard and understood.

The seven churches in Revelation would not have been afraid of straight speaking. If there had been more straight speaking among themselves, they may not have needed Jesus to write to them so bluntly via John. We can imagine the leader from Pergamum speaking up particularly strongly on this point, conscious of how helpful it would have been to have had a Concerned Church call them out on some of the compromised teachings they had allowed to circulate among their members.[179]

In inter-church circles today, straight speaking can often be one-sided. We sense that those who have spoken out strongly to us will not appreciate us speaking out strongly to them in return, and sadly in some cases we may be right. We live in a world where some of us think it acceptable to cancel out views that do not align with our own, claiming them to be invalid even before they are properly presented. But remaining silent solves nothing. We may think that by saying nothing we are being kind, but it could be that we are just being timid or miscalculating. In thinking that a Concerned Church would prefer

178. Galatians 2:4.
179. Revelation 2:12-15.

to have no pushbacks, we could be doing it a disservice. It may not be thinking like that at all. In writing, the Revelation leaders will want to encourage a Concerned Church to speak out as boldly as Paul did in Antioch, but they would also be aware of how exceedingly blunt Jesus was when addressing them via John on Patmos. We need to remember that the cross is God's instrument of reconciliation and that nothing about the cross is comfortable.

One further thought can be best presented to us by the leaders from Smyrna and Philadelphia. They need to be brought in to speak about tenacity. They would want to point out that their churches, the only two to be commended without being corrected, were not being tenacious in just holding to their own opinions. Smyrna was encouraged to maintain its faithful stand for truth in the face of slander, no matter how costly it would prove for some.[180] Philadelphia was up against similar challenges but was promised a breakthrough. Its letter emphasised the nature of its faithfulness: 'I know that you have little strength, yet you have kept my word and not denied my name.'[181]

The 'word' they kept is probably best understood as the teaching given to the Church by the Twelve after Pentecost. At the end of the first century, this was already beginning to be circulated in written form by Matthew, Mark, Luke and John and was being clarified in letters by Paul and others of the apostles. 'Not denying the name' was a way of referring to never abandoning personal faith in Christ, no matter how great the pressure to back away from such a wholehearted commitment. By contrast it is clear that some of the Revelation churches were coming close to a denial of Christ's name, if only through mixing a once-strong commitment either with false teaching or with a love for the ways of the world. The example set by Philadelphia in keeping Christ's word and

---

180. Revelation 2:9-11.
181. Revelation 3:7-10.

not denying his name is important in terms of focus for a Concerned Church today.

Let's see what a letter from the leaders of the seven Revelation churches might say.

To the Concerned Church

[Try reading this aloud in the way the church leaders in Revelation would have read out their letters.]

Greetings from your fellow churches that have gone before you and have known Christ commending those among us who have held firmly to his word and honoured his name, while correcting those of us who have wavered.

We are one with you in your desire to see truth upheld and ask you, for everyone's sake, not to take your convictions lightly or to hold back in expressing them. Maintaining truth has to be the responsibility of us all. The Church as a whole will only be able to bring the full brightness of its light to the world when every church is fully committed to God's truth and justice. We are confident that you know this and we respect your concern for your fellow churches.

We are aware that there appear to be times when you might think it kinder to walk away from those who disagree with you and to step aside from those who seem not to share your passion. This is an understandable reaction if it is motivated by anxieties about compromising truth or devaluing firmly held principles. But surely such protectiveness runs the risk of undervaluing both the truth and the principles it seeks to safeguard. Should not such truth and principles be able to withstand the rigours that arise in any arena where they are granted entry? If a conviction we hold proves to be less than the truth, or turns out to be a substandard principle, surely it is better to discover this. We are saying this from experience. We all need to be open to reassess in the course of honest debate.

We urge you to learn from us. Engaging with one another will enable the truth of the gospel and the unfailing justice of God to be expressed more widely and upheld more confidently. The light we carry is part of a greater light, and we know only too well that there have been times when the light some of us have carried has not proved to have been sparked by God's will or affirmed in his Word. Press on. We know that those who are getting it right are not always the ones that are noisiest about their convictions, but nonetheless this does not take away the responsibility of contending vocally for the truth. In this we appreciate your stand.

There is a unity that Christ has given us through the cross that is sufficient to facilitate vigorous debate and righteous outcomes. If we embrace this in all humility, truth and justice will be the beneficiaries and the light we as churches bring to the world will shine even more brightly.

Challenge:

Write two ways in which you would proactively respond to such a letter if you were a member of a church like this.

1.

2.

11. Finding a Forum

The Jerusalem church has matured. We can see that it is no longer focused on thousands gathering daily in Solomon's Porch. Nonetheless, Jerusalem is still full of Jewish visitors for the feasts and these provide an opportunity for the church to engage with the crowds. The rest of the time, however, there is a settled congregation of Jerusalem residents accompanied from time to time by their visitors.

James is a permanent presence, with some fellow elders around him. Peter and John, and possibly others from the Twelve, continue to come and go. The make-up of the church reflects the make-up of Jerusalem. It is a major religious city, and some who are part of its religious structures are also part of the church.[182] It is not without its challenges from Roman officials and religious authorities, but it feels more settled and has some advantages. The fact that Jerusalem remains a centre for receiving visitors means that the church has a working knowledge of what is happening, not only throughout the Jewish diaspora but across the Gentile world. With genuine grace, the Jerusalem church accepts that it is no longer unique in the Christian world and that God has been doing things for which it cannot take credit, and over which it has no control.

In many ways the meeting that takes place in Jerusalem, as recorded in Acts 15, is, from a unity perspective, the highlight of the first-century narrative. It not only shows the Church's determination to face up to problems, but indicates an underlying strength of unity that enables challenges to be tackled with confidence. But as the group from Antioch journeys towards Jerusalem, negative comments about James tend to creep into their conversations. Paul and Barnabas are aware of this but steer clear of getting involved.[183] They know that the circumcision

---

182. Acts 6:7.
183. Galatians 2:12.

advocates mentioned James by name when in Antioch, but they have no intention of making things personal when they get to the city.

Amazingly, on arrival the risk disappears in an instant. The welcome from the Jerusalem church is overwhelming.[184] The undeniable warmth in the relationship between the Jerusalem believers and Paul and Barnabas takes the rest of the party from Antioch by surprise. The excitement increases as more and more people turn up to receive them. Peter and James are there, as are those whom the two of them have come to trust locally as their fellow elders.

News of Barnabas and Paul's arrival continues to spread. There is a real buzz as everyone presses around them to hear about Antioch and their travels around Galatia. As Paul gives his report, there is not the slightest hint of the awkwardness his fellow travellers have been anticipating: no mutterings, no rebukes, no legalistic murmurings. This feels like unity at its best. Greatly reassured, those from Antioch exchange glances, nods and smiles. As Gentile believers, they had expected to be marginalised. But as Paul draws his report to a close with people still arriving, a few believing Pharisees make their presence known. Sadly, they seem unable to distinguish between the traditional legalistic procedure of accepting converts into Judaism and the spiritual process of seeing people turn to Christ. They speak out, insisting that the Gentiles they have just heard Paul speak about must be circumcised and told to keep the law.[185]

The atmosphere changes in an instant, but wisely Paul does not rise to the bait. James knows why he and Barnabas have come, and Paul has to trust that James has things in hand. The heckling quickly dies down and friendly conversations pick up from where they were before Paul began. Clearly there are some big underlying issues in Jerusalem, and although unity is obviously the reality that almost everyone is keen to see and quick to celebrate, a measure of embarrassment lies beneath the surface.

---

184. Acts 15:4.
185. Acts 15:5.

Eventually they get down to business. The circumcision matter is to be discussed with James and Peter and with those who share the responsibility for overseeing the Jerusalem church. But that does not stop a large group of local believers staying around to listen. The topic is one that concerns them all and they are not going to be left out. They are all aware that somehow the church in Jerusalem has ended up at the heart of the matter. They know they have a wide range of opinions among their number. There are those who are keen to express their new-found faith in Christ in the context of their Jewish religious culture, which presents no problem as long as they know they are not saved by keeping the Law of Moses, even if they still choose to follow it. Others, who may not be quite so clear on these basics, believe that the law should be applied more widely and a few of them have become quite vocal about it – hence the heckling the day before.

When the meeting begins, the focus initially is on these local issues. And it feels as if this is not the first time the problems have been discussed. The observers from Antioch quickly discover that the challenge goes right back to the beginning, when the new believers in Jerusalem worked hard to make sure that the division between traditional Jews and Hellenistic Jews did not split the church.[186] It seems that for years some Jews have preferred to stay with Jewish practices while others have accepted Greek culture and had a far more liberal approach to the law. The question of how to handle the Gentile believers seems to feed into this long-running cultural tension. Obviously, with Jerusalem being at the centre of Judaism, it is more of a problem here than further afield. It all makes for interesting listening, but something has to happen to widen out the discussion. As the local leaders talk, they are skirting around theological issues. Paul listens in silence. He has thought all of this through and has set out all of his reasoning for the Galatians, but

---

186. Acts 6:1-2.

he knows that it is a heart change and not a head change that is needed right now.

Not surprisingly it is Peter who gets to his feet to break the impasse. His contribution is short, simple and practical. He refers everyone back to how God gave the Holy Spirit in Cornelius' house, pointing out that God's approach is to treat everyone equally. He asks why, if God accepts the Gentiles just as they are, should they be burdened with rules that every Jew finds hard to keep? He retakes his seat, having neatly turned the argument on its head. In effect he has jolted everyone's thinking by hinting that the challenge is actually more about Jews becoming like Gentiles than Gentiles becoming like Jews. It is Peter at his bluntest and his best.[187]

The tension slowly eases and the frowns turn to smiles. James raises his eyebrows and nods to Paul and Barnabas. The three of them seem to know that this is not the moment to resolve the theological issues Peter has so neatly sidestepped. He has brought everything back to the sovereignty of God and they are free to speak. It is time for everyone to hear more about Gentiles coming to faith and the signs and wonders God has done in the Gentile world. They start on Cyprus with the spiritual battle in the home of the proconsul,[188] and lead on to the breakthrough with the Gentiles at Antioch in Pisidia, and Iconium.[189] In particular the healing at Lystra holds everyone's attention, especially when they hear how the local crowd switched from worshipping Paul and Barnabas to stoning Paul.[190] They gasp as Paul says that after he had been left for dead the new believers 'gathered round him' and saw him back on his feet.[191]

---

187. Acts 15:7-11.
188. Acts 13:6-12.
189. Acts 13:13 – 14:7.
190. Acts 24:8-18.
191. Acts 14:19-20.

No one could deny that God must have been at work to raise up such faith-filled Gentile believers.[192]

James stands to draw the session to a close. He speaks from his heart. It is God who has taken the initiative with the Gentiles, having made his plans to include them known through the prophets. It would be wrong to make things difficult for Gentiles turning to Christ. Unity can be maintained by telling them to keep themselves from food offered to idols, from immorality, 'from the meat of strangled animals and from blood'.[193] A letter needs to be crafted, but in agreeing to this, the Jerusalem believers decide to send more than a letter. Writing can make it clear to those in Antioch, Syria and Cilicia that the people who disturbed them were wrong in saying they were sent by James and the Jerusalem church, but sending some church members would make the point even more apologetically. They choose two, one of whom is Silas, who later will travel extensively with Paul.[194]

The letter is written and the representatives sent on their way. The Jerusalem church has gained some clarity and had the privilege of setting things in place for generations to come. With this in mind it is a good point to break off and consider a letter to the Courteous Church.

Let's now take a moment to reflect on some key points that we can take forward:

- Having to host the Church's first Council with one side in the dispute (falsely) claiming to have the endorsement of James was not easy for the Jerusalem church. How did it conduct itself to see an agreement reached that seemed good to the Holy Spirit and to all who were present?

---

192. Acts 15:12.
193. Acts 15:13-21.
194. Acts 15:22-29.

- Peter spoke of the even-handedness of the Holy Spirit being poured out on the first Gentile believers in the same way as he had been on the Jewish believers at Pentecost. How should we take account of the Holy Spirit's work in the lives of those being called into question today?

- The Council did not pass personal judgement on the members of the circumcision party, although it clearly refuted their views and denied that the Church had endorsed them.[195] Did this go far enough, given that Paul was willing to question if the members of the circumcision party were true believers?

- Although the Council decision allowed Jewish practices to continue for Jewish believers but not for Gentile believers, there were still some areas where Gentiles were required to be sensitive to Jewish views. Did this lead to a twin-track Church or reflect what Church unity should really be like?

---

195. Acts 15:24.

12. Letter to the Courteous Church

There is little doubt that we would all want a church that holds a privileged position in society to be courteous. In countries where there is an established Church, the privileges in society may come automatically to those local churches within it, but it is still good to assume privilege and courtesy should always go hand-in-hand. As we define a Courteous Church, we will stay with the idea of it being a church that is privileged, and simply identify the characteristics that will need to be brought to the fore to help it in such a role.

St Peter's is right in the centre of our imaginary town, taking up most of the north side of the market square. The War Memorial Gardens are situated right next to it, adding to its civic significance. The church predates the War Memorial by several centuries, at least in part. Internally it has gone through a complete reordering, with much of the dark wood removed, leaving it far more light and airy on the inside than the outside might imply. Even the town's nonconformist churches find it quite a conducive environment, and the rector who oversaw the reordering is still the incumbent, just as uncomplicated and uncluttered in her approach as the church's interior – friendly and welcoming to all. The mayor and council love her, and although in other towns, civic services are normally limited to a short annual visit to the War Memorial, St Peter's is happy to host an inauguration service at the start of the municipal year, and also an annual civic carol service. The town sees it as its church.

Getting all the other churches in town to see St Peter's in such a way has never been that easy, and the rector is constantly assuring the rest of the town's clergy that she has no grandiose ideas about her role. In her mind, the minister of Station Road has equal authority along with the leadership of Life Church, the vicar of St Saviour's, the elders of Ebenezer Hall and the new minister at Glad Tidings. Working this out in practice is more difficult. Her idea of an annual pulpit exchange does not fill everyone with enthusiasm. Nonetheless, that doesn't stop the vicar of St Saviour's suggesting that maybe the doctor who leads the multicultural fellowship should be included in the exchange. The rector smiles. Clearly there is still more work to be done, and she knows that goes for her own congregation too, some of whom worship at St Peter's precisely because they appreciate the social prestige and believe it to be a cut above the rest.

Portraying the rector of St Peter's as so inclusive is helpful since it reminds us that a Courteous Church must always be aware that when it speaks to local government, it has to speak on behalf of all the Christians within the council's area. Knowing this, it will recognise the importance of gleaning first-hand information about all the other local churches. How much effort it puts into this will, to some degree, define the extent of its courtesy. Having said this, other local churches may from time to time covet its privileged position, but in practice, shifting responsibility from the shoulders of one church onto another will achieve little. Civic leaders do not have the time or inclination to consult widely, and if another church shouts so loudly that it comes to be preferred, it will simply become the new representative and face the same responsibilities. In the end, being a Courteous Church is not about having a profile, and certainly not about assuming it is expressing kindness by being patronising, but about being inclusive, gracious and effective.

We will almost certainly have realised that a Courteous Church, if wise, will want to establish an information-sharing forum. To do this, it may have to take a lead among its fellow churches. If it does so, it will work best if it approaches other churches graciously, not relying on its denominational status or any history it may have acquired. Nevertheless, a long history can add a sense of stability, and a church that is secure in its own identity can provide an important local anchor point. In the end, it is the church's ability to be a good listener and a faithful representative that really counts.

Showing a humble acceptance of its privileged position will also assist. The Jerusalem church proved to be the go-to place at a time of dispute, not only because the people causing trouble claimed to carry its authority but because it was secure enough to allow everyone space to speak and room to be heard. This is the essence of a Courteous Church: showing understanding and openness to all. If we are going to see effective and robust local inter-church relationships, we will need many Courteous Churches to step forward without the slightest hint of being patronising.

In encouraging a Courteous Church, we need to explore the challenges it could face in fulfilling its role. A good starting point would be to look at the risks that go with a sense of entitlement. Sadly, there is a kind of courtesy that can leave others feeling demeaned and patronised rather than respected as equals. Nothing is guaranteed to kill inter-church relationships more quickly than such condescending kindness. If the leaders of the church in Ephesus were still to have a copy of the letter Paul sent to Corinth when he was with them, they might offer us his illustration of how the body fits together as a useful template for inter-church relations. No church, let alone a Courteous Church, should ever say to another congregation 'we have no need of you' or to allow a church to feel so marginalised that it ends up saying 'we do not belong'.[196] A Courteous Church should make all local churches feel properly valued and help them to benefit fully from each other's strengths.

Now if a sense of entitlement could be a challenge, so could complacency. In fact, they often go hand-in-hand. If the leaders from Ephesus could contribute Paul's illustration to the Corinthians to counter complacency, maybe the leaders from Sardis could reflect on

---

196. 1 Corinthians 12:12-27.

how their church became dead while still being seen as alive.[197] That must have involved a lot of complacency. Hopefully the few in Sardis whom Jesus commended for staying alive were strong enough to turn their church around.[198] Our hope is that a Courteous Church, especially one with a long history, will always have enough enthusiastic people in it to stop complacency stifling its energy.

A lively, welcoming Courteous Church that gets to know its fellow churches will be genuinely appreciated, even by those that consider themselves to be livelier, louder or larger. We need to keep this in mind as we weigh the likely thoughts of the leaders of the seven Revelation church leaders.

---

197. Revelation 3:1.
198. Revelation 3:4-5.

To the Courteous Church

[Try reading this aloud in the way the church leaders in Revelation would have read out their letters.]

Greetings from your fellow churches that have gone before you and came to appreciate inclusiveness and learned the wisdom of maintaining a generous spirit.

We congratulate you on your faithfulness that enables you to speak on behalf of others. We know that gaining such respect comes at a price, and we commend you for establishing the links that make it possible to represent others accurately. You know that many of us do not have your profile or connectivity within society but, like you, our hearts are set on being faithful so that together we can make an impact.

We recall the needs in our own localities and can see how helpful it must be to have access to elected policymakers. It must be challenging to help them understand that although we serve the same people we, as the Church, are seeking to change lives spiritually and not just socially. Nonetheless, they need to know the breadth of the activities that you and your fellow churches are engaged in and the full extent of your concerns.

We know that working with each other requires sensitivity and that maintaining confidence between each other is actually more important than maintaining the confidence of those outside the Church. We urge you to embrace your inter-church calling at least as strongly and effectively as you embrace your public role, and to lay aside any sense of entitlement or denominational superiority that might lead to an undermining of others in local church leadership.

We know that additional responsibilities can weigh on a church and we want your light in the community to be bright. We know that the light shines brightest when we all shine together, so we pray that your light will never be eclipsed by overfamiliarity with formal worship or the weight of history, and certainly not by the responsibility of having to speak on behalf of all.

We urge you to walk relationally, aware that at any time you may be called upon by your fellow churches to provide a safe place for robust debate. May your graciousness be matched by your wisdom at such times, and may God grant you levels of understanding that enable every other local believer to know that they are rightly appreciated as equals in the kingdom of God. We can learn from one another, even from those who think and act differently.

May your generosity and courtesy speak of the security of your relationship with our living Saviour.

Challenge:

Write two ways in which you would proactively respond to such a letter if you were a member of a church like this.

1.

2.

13. Correction and Care

Some months have passed since Paul and Barnabas returned from Jerusalem with Judas and Silas, and it is a while since Paul sent his letter to the Galatians. The churches there are yet to receive the letter agreed on in Jerusalem. He is keen to visit them and to encourage them face to face. He plans to go via Cilicia, his home area, where he lived and preached before Barnabas brought him to Antioch. He begins to talk to Barnabas about an overland trip. Barnabas raises the possibility of John Mark coming with them, but Paul refuses. The young man walked away during their previous journey and in Paul's eyes has yet to prove himself worthy of a second chance. Barnabas thinks differently, and after a sharp disagreement they decide to go their separate ways. Barnabas takes John Mark back to Cyprus, the scene of the young man's earlier failures. Paul invites Silas to travel with him.[199]

This kind of disruption may not sit comfortably with those seeking unity today, but it would not have been out of place in the first-century Church where a robust unity was upheld with confidence. We have seen that an equal commitment to truth, pastoral care and unity can produce an environment where convictions can be expressed without compromise and correction can go hand-in-hand with care. The split between Paul and Barnabas was over someone who needed both care and correction. Paul was not being hard-hearted towards John Mark in disciplining him, any more than Barnabas was being dismissive of the need to 'sort the young man out' while he was encouraging him. Their contention may have been sharp but their convictions were clear. And no one in Antioch appears to have stepped in to offer any counselling to the two of them. There are times when things should be allowed to take their course, trusting in everyone's maturity. The incident obviously left

---

199. Acts 15:36-41.

Paul with no hang-ups about working with younger leaders. By the time he reaches Lystra he is ready to recruit Timothy.[200]

Timothy's introduction to travelling with Paul and Silas is very different from John Mark's experience of accompanying Barnabas and Paul. Having revisited the cities known to Paul from his earlier visit, they move on from Galatia with no particular destination in mind. They want to break fresh ground, but no doors seem to be opening. Eventually they reach Troas on the coast. It is here that Paul has a vision that takes them to Macedonia.[201]

They head for Philippi, where progress seems slow at first but is ultimately fruitful, despite (or perhaps because of) Paul and Silas' brief imprisonment. From there it is on to Thessalonica and Berea, before Paul travels ahead of them to Athens. After he has spent some time on his own in Athens, he moves to Corinth.[202] This is where we reconnect with our early Church narrative and pick up more fully on our theme of correction and care.

Before Silas and Timothy join Paul in Corinth, they are delayed in Macedonia because Paul has sent Timothy back from Berea to settle his anxieties over the new church in Thessalonica. But now they have arrived in Corinth and Paul is able to write to the Thessalonians on the basis of Timothy's update. He does this as he starts his ministry in Corinth, highlighting the importance he will be placing on letter-writing from now on. His letter to the church in Thessalonica, like his earlier one to the Galatians, is full of love and concern.[203] Little did the Corinthians know that one day Paul would be writing to them as part of his commitment to bringing care and correction throughout the early Church.

---

200. Acts 16:1-3.
201. Acts 16:6-9.
202. Acts 16:10 – 18:1.
203. 1 Thessalonians 2:17 – 3:10.

From day one in Corinth Paul finds himself very much at home. He moves in with Aquila and Priscilla, fellow tentmakers, who have recently escaped the persecution of Jews in Rome. Within days he is teaching in the synagogue. People are responsive but when Timothy and Silas arrive and he becomes more adamant in stating that Jesus is the Christ, the Jews oppose him and he goes next door to hold meetings for the Gentiles. Ironically, it is at this point that the synagogue leader and his family become believers. This opens the way for many others to believe and Paul is encouraged by God to stay for a further eighteen months. He establishes a church with a character that comes across clearly in the letters he sends them later.[204]

We can probably sum up the Corinthian church in five words: diverse, expressive, confident, zealous and generous. Paul eventually has to write to its members on each of these points. He loves the diversity at Corinth. People are coming to follow Jesus from backgrounds that might leave some of us who have been overly sheltered relieved not to be worshipping in the same local church. They are all, as Paul writes, washed, sanctified and justified, and many are glad they will never again be seeing the inside of a law court.[205]

Some in Corinth, though, have yet to work out how to solve their problems without going before the magistrates, and this is something Paul has to correct.[206] On top of this it is a very vocal church, and speaking up in court is not the only place where church members are likely to be heard. Speaking out in the middle of church gatherings is something they all seem to do with great enthusiasm. Their meetings are full of lively contributions as everyone wants to bring what they believe the Holy Spirit has given them to say.[207] Paul has to remind

---

204. Acts 18:2-17.
205. 1 Corinthians 6:9-11.
206. 1 Corinthians 6:1-8
207. 1 Corinthians 14:26-40.

them that 'God is not a God of disorder but of peace'.[208] It is a correction graciously given.

No one can be around the Corinthian church for long without noticing its confidence and zeal, and there are times when its confidence seems to know no bounds. On occasions it can even threaten to be divisive. The members are so keen to develop their own style of worship that Paul has to remind them how other churches function. Internally they almost split over whether they should look to Paul, Peter or Apollos for their authority, with the more superior ones then trying to trump them all by claiming that they look to Christ.[209]

Paul points out that they may think that this kind of behaviour reveals their confidence, but in reality it exposes their immaturity.[210] The same is true when later he has to show them that although they may consider themselves to be discerning, they are inadvertently opening up the church to so-called apostles who are not really apostles at all.[211] Strangely enough, some of these false apostles seem to have been restricting their spiritual freedom,[212] even though rule-keeping is not generally the Corinthian way.

Corinthian believers are in fact quite likely to try to show their liberty even more extravagantly than the society around them. No one in the church seems to have any qualms when the women in the congregation decide to break local cultural norms by abandoning their head coverings. Paul has to point out that going bare-headed in their culture is just one step away from having their heads shaved, which is the local punishment for prostitution.[213]

---

208. 1 Corinthians 14:33.
209. 1 Corinthians 1:10-13.
210. 1 Corinthians 3:1-4.
211. 2 Corinthians 11:5-15.
212. 2 Corinthians 11:20.
213. 1 Corinthians 11:1-16.

Trying to see things through the eyes of others is not the church's strong point. Some Corinthian believers feel unsure about eating cheap cuts of meat from the market that have been offered to idols. Those who have no such concerns tend to go ahead without giving anyone else a thought. Paul has to tell them that respecting each other's conscience is more important than displaying confidence.[214] The Corinthians may seem slow to learn but they can also be zealous to comply. Even with this they may go too far. The man who has to be put out of the church for a season because of his immorality almost never gets back in, despite his repentance, all because the church is determined not to be labelled as too half-hearted in its discipline.[215]

Paul obviously loves this church. He warms to its enthusiasm, despite all of the corrections he has to bring. He knows it is a generous church and he wants it to contribute to a gift that he is gathering for the church in Jerusalem. True to form, they commit early. Sadly, they are then rather slow to deliver.[216] In addressing this, Paul provides an excellent example of how to balance correction and care: 'But since you excel in everything – in faith, in speech, in knowledge, in complete earnestness and in the love we have kindled in you – see that you also excel in this grace of giving.'[217] I think he writes this with a smile on his face, knowing that he is reflecting back to them the very image that they somewhat arrogantly hold of themselves.

Love in the first-century Church was strong and the unity was robust enough to handle correction, no matter how frequently it had to be given or how widely it had to be applied. It is worth keeping this in mind as we consider a letter from the seven Revelation leaders to a Confident Church today.

---

214. 1 Corinthians 8:1-13.
215. 1 Corinthians 5:1-13; 2 Corinthians 2:3-11.
216. 2 Corinthians 8:1 - 9:15.
217. 2 Corinthians 8:7.

Let's now take a moment to reflect on some key points that we can take forward:

- Paul's second missionary journey began with a dispute over John Mark. Barnabas and Paul used a combination of encouragement and discipline to help him. How can we achieve the right balance when mentoring young individuals and young congregations?
- Paul recruited Timothy soon after turning down Mark. What does this show us about Paul's character and approach to ministry?
- Paul arrives in Philippi in response to a call for help given in a dream. How significant is the word 'help' in the way Paul raises the church there?
- When we look at the church in Corinth, we see an energetic congregation. In what way does its confidence serve it well and in what ways does it hinder?

14. Letter to the Confident Church

So we arrive at our final letter and it is going to be to a Confident Church. The Corinthian church has given us an insight into what a Confident Church looked like in the first century. We now have to consider what one looks like in the twenty-first century.

Fresh Hope Community Church is the newest church in town, still not quite six years old. The young couple who lead it were part of a similar congregation in a city nearby, and were asked to consider planting a church in our imaginary town to cater for those who had been travelling ten miles there and back every Sunday. It had been growing quickly as the initial families and young couples recruited other young couples, families and young people who liked the idea of the informality and intimacy of a smaller gathering. They have met in the same school for five years now but have gradually had to ask permission to use more classrooms as the work with the younger children has grown, although they make sure that those who are fourteen and over feel at home in the main service, knowing that they are supported by a youth pastor, employed part-time by the church, during the week.

Being aware of Fresh Hope's newness, the lead couple and the youth pastor try to make it to as many inter-church meetings as possible. Of the three of them, the youth pastor is probably the most excitable and outspoken, constantly enthusing about what Fresh Hope is doing. The founding couple encourage him to hold the floor as they are trying to break a mould and believe that in a restrained environment some effusive overselling may not go amiss. They are also aware that their church is on a journey to maturity, a journey that they hope will always be marked by excited and excitable newcomers. In their enthusiasm they seem blind to the half-hearted reception they receive, reading a level of interest into the smiles and nods that might be more accurately interpreted as bored dismissal. Such lack of awareness is something that they will need to address.

We definitely need more churches that are as confident as Fresh Hope – confident in the gospel, confident in the plan of God and confident in their calling. But how much of an inspiration a Confident Church can be to other churches will depend on its attitude. Looking back to first-century Corinth, we see a church that seems to have been excellent at inspiring confidence among its members. People were encouraged to speak out and say what they believed God was telling them. Nothing could have been more positive than that in inspiring people to have a strong personal relationship with God. However, confidence eventually ran so high in Corinth that every contribution was taken at face value. No time was set aside to weigh what was being said.[218]

It is amazing that a church raised up by someone as careful in his public statements as Paul should so readily have seemed to have abandoned the depth of study, the reliance on Scripture, and the willingness to submit everything to review that must have characterised its early gatherings. But this is where confidence can cover a lack of maturity. Paul's corrective pointed them in the direction of collective wisdom and effective discipleship. Anyone can speak but everyone must weigh what has been said, and everybody needs a growing understanding in order to weigh things effectively. A church that fails to have these safeguards in place in its congregational setting is likely to adopt the same overconfident attitude when building inter-church relationships and engaging with wider society. A Confident Church can often be a 'what-you-see-is-what-you-get' church. While some may find this ability to present its current thinking so vigorously and spontaneously to be really refreshing, others will register its lack of depth, its unthought-through content and, sometimes, its cultural inappropriateness.

---

218. 1 Corinthians 14:29-32.

Few churches today have the open platform that was given to everyone at Corinth, but churches still have their business meetings and attend inter-church gatherings and these are still occasions when confident presentations can cause tensions. A Confident Church is unlikely to be standoffish and will be more than happy when gathering with others to share its latest news. It will definitely bring its own energy to every gathering. Paul loved the enthusiasm of the church at Corinth despite its occasional displays of overconfidence, and believed that with skill and grace its abundant energy could be harnessed. He was careful never to undermine its confidence or restrict the extent of its members' participation. In fact, he encouraged both.

Even so, he worked sensitively to curb what, at the time, were its cultural indiscretions and sought to expose and remove any underlying tendencies to dominate. If it had not been for Paul's fatherly intervention, neither of these problems would have been obvious to the church. Paul was not interested in dampening down enthusiasm so much as wanting to know there were checks and balances. He understood that a Confident Church can be enthusiastic about almost anything, but when it comes to being confident about almost everything, this is not always wise.

Today information bombards us from every side. We are never short of strongly argued options to embrace. Enthusiastic adopters can be sold out on a critical view on an issue in the morning and hold a positive view on the same matter in the afternoon. Equally, there are now so many shades of biblical interpretation online, and so many analyses of political events and social trends, that we can chop and change our opinions on almost anything. This can be really confusing. At one moment a Confident Church can be holding a position so determinedly that it is like a child putting its fingers in its ears and boasting, 'I'm right, you're wrong.' The next moment, when something trendier and more current comes along, it can be jumping on the latest bandwagon and telling everyone to come on board too. Both of these are marks of immaturity.

To bring about a shift from overconfidence to confidence at Corinth, Paul opened up the issue of spiritual maturity. Maturity in the Christian world comes to those who seek it rather than to those who just hope it arrives as time goes by, and maturity is not the same as steadiness. Things are actually at their most steady when everything is at a standstill. Paul was determined that the Church should mature without losing momentum. Steadiness for its own sake was never his goal, either locally or globally. We must be equally determined to maintain pace when considering confidence, maturity and momentum today if we are to avoid stagnation in the twenty-first-century Church.

The churches in Revelation might have some further light to shed on the whole issue of maturity. For a season they were all growing to maturity. Seeing some of them throw all of that away and revert to naïvely thinking they had already arrived must have been heart-breaking. God wants us to go forwards, not backwards. Their repentance no doubt saw their maturity restored, and a willingness to learn from mistakes could even have added to it. If they had stayed on track, they could have replicated the pattern John introduced in one of the letters he had written while with them.

In what we call his first letter, John acknowledges that the Church is made up of spiritual youths, spiritual babies and those who are spiritually mature. He even enthusiastically congratulates spiritual youths, saying 'you are strong, and the word of God lives in you, and you have overcome the evil one'.[219] These are powerful words and display an incredible amount of gracious affirmation on John's part. If the members of the seven churches had all retained the confidence they knew in their spiritual youth, rather than regressing or straying into complacency, they could have reached a level of spiritual maturity more readily. The

219. 1 John 2:12-14.

Laodicean leadership would surely have been of this view.[220] Their church had clearly lost its early zeal and must somehow have suppressed the natural zeal of its younger members. A restored Laodicean church would definitely want to speak out against any suppression of youthful zeal.

A Confident Church needs to know that the encouragement and acceptance it extends to its congregational members can be theirs in inter-church circles if they can find a way of sharing their encouragement with humility. When the Revelation churches were building again after slipping back into spiritual infancy, they would have had to rediscover their early, 'youthful' characteristics of strength, scriptural dependence and victorious authority. Confidence has its place on the path to maturity and a Confident Church, pressing on to maturity, can bring momentum to the wider Church world, countering the stagnation that some mistake for maturity.

So, let's see how the seven Revelation churches, now restored, can help us ensure zeal is never missing from our interconnectivity.

---

220. Revelation 3:14-19.

To the Confident Church

[Try reading this aloud in the way the church leaders in Revelation would have read out their letters.]

Greetings from your fellow churches that have gone before and discovered afresh the value of momentum and enthusiasm. We celebrate your confidence in the gospel and in your calling, and appreciate your willingness to share your thoughts and priorities with others. Do not be dismayed if at times they express their endorsement with caution. It is good to mix confidence with humility, and presenting your thoughts and priorities in a reasoned way will help everyone weigh them and benefit from them. While the ground on which you stand may be firm, others around you will know of other ground that is less so. It is good to learn from their experience and not to despise their wisdom.

When our churches began, we saw how the freshness of our enthusiasm halted the spiritual decline in our communities. We encourage you to keep your expression of church fresh, as it will help others overcome unnecessary reservations. Do this with sensitivity and it will allow respect for each other to grow.

We understand that you have many young Christians with a strong grasp of their personal salvation who are starting out on their faith journey. We urge you to keep developing ways to see their understanding and commitment deepen. We have heard that you bring a high-energy mix of presentation, participation and performance to your worship services – make sure you also include in them a thorough and consistent Bible-teaching programme.

We all now know what Jesus said to the two churches among us in which he found no fault – he spoke to Smyrna of its faithfulness and to Philadelphia of it having kept his word and not denied his name.[221]

---

221. Revelation 3:8.

Young believers need to be able to move on from milk to meat without losing interest or waning in their enthusiasm.

Finally we want to stress the importance of building together. If your confidence enables you to present your thoughts and enthusiasm in a way that brings a multiplication of trust, and your discipleship programmes bring maturity to your members, the credibility you carry will be truly inspiring and will greatly increase the joint impact of the Church across your local community.

Challenge:
Write two ways in which you would proactively respond to such a letter if you were a member of a church like this.

1.

2.

15. Pursuing the Ultimate

In our opening chapter we said a little about ultimate unity, seeing it as the unity presented to us in the heavenly Jerusalem, the bride of Christ.[222] We also mentioned how Paul differentiated between the unity of the Spirit that we have and must keep 'through the bond of peace', and the unity in the faith that we need to be equipped to reach.[223] I am confident that when we as churches keep the unity of the Spirit by engaging wholeheartedly with one another in the practical ways we have considered, we are actually working towards unity in the faith. I will not be dismayed, though, if we are not one on all matters of belief and practice before Jesus returns, as I know that our efforts will have contributed to our corporate maturity.

The good news is that when we stand in God's presence, all our differences of belief and practice will be of no consequence. We shall all believe rightly as we will finally see all things with absolute clarity. We will not even bother to check among ourselves to see who was the most right and who was the most wrong. There will be greater joys in heaven than point-scoring over past theological deliberations.

Nonetheless, it is good to keep on clarifying our convictions and examining how we put them into practice. After all, these things affect our spiritual development and evangelistic effectiveness. While we are on earth, it is our joint commitment to spiritual maturity, our zeal in evangelism and our unswerving devotion to Christ that will see the enemy finally defeated: 'They [the faithful believers] triumphed over him [the devil, the accuser] by the blood of the Lamb and by the word of their testimony; they did not love their lives so much as to shrink from death.'[224] The simplicity of walking together faithfully in truth and love,

---

222. Revelation 21:9-10.
223. Ephesians 4:3,11-16.
224. Revelation 12:11.

addressing our differences boldly and respectfully in humility and hope, will surely prove as effective as it is exciting: 'If we walk in the light, as he is in the light, we have fellowship with one another, and the blood of Jesus, his Son, purifies us from all sin.'[225]

I know Christ is returning for a bride 'without spot and wrinkle',[226] and he is working on our perfection with heavenly preparations taking place too.[227] In my mind the heavenly preparations must be as practical as our earthly ones, and just as focused on completion as they were when God determined them in heaven before the beginning of time.

The reality is that this spotless, unwrinkled bride will have to be gathered from across the centuries and not just from some future (or maybe even present) final generation. This is way beyond our ability to imagine. The generations of the past may inspire us or dismay us. At times different pictures have been in our predecessors' minds, and some of these pictures might have borne little relation to the Church as it was in the beginning. That, though, is not our responsibility. We have an opportunity to make an impact in our day and it will be all the stronger if we overcome the challenges we have highlighted – the dilution of unconditional love, the downplaying of zeal, the withdrawal into self-sufficiency, the drift towards superficiality, the retreat from necessary argument and the tendency to engage patronisingly or presumptuously, all of which can be misrepresented as kindness. They are all approaches that have to go.

So let us remind ourselves of the great coming together of all things that lies ahead of us. In the book of Revelation, we not only see the heavenly city but are shown its myriad of inhabitants, drawn from 'every nation, tribe, people and language', worshipping God as one.[228] And I believe if we look closely, we will find that the tribes and people-groups,

---

225. 1 John 1:7.
226. Ephesians 5:27, ESV.
227. Revelation 19:7; 21:2.
228. Revelation 7:9-17.

although still individually identifiable despite their white robes, are not standing in their expected groupings, and neither are the separate denominations assembled in theirs. The battle to uphold truth, unity and godly character in the face of three-fold pressures from a fallen world, the challenge of unbridled passions and the distractions of a devious devil will have been utterly and indisputably won.[229] We will be celebrating God's greatness together in a unity that has no need for cliques or clusters.

In that place of rest and victory, we probably will not want for one moment to take our eyes off God in his glory – the blaze of his light will be so bright and our corporate focus on him will be so strong.[230] But if we were to look around, we would see once again how well the city has been built. The walls are strong, raised on the foundational teaching laid down by the twelve apostles at and after Pentecost.[231] Despite the pressures, the years have been kind, enabling faithful expositors of God's Word through the centuries to keep building until the final call. We need not check to see if there are stones that represent our contribution, but we should be concerned if much of what our generation has built turns out to be 'wood, hay or straw'.[232]

If we were to look a little further, we would see the gates wide open,[233] and we could pause to recognise that they have been kept that way by congregations across the millennia that, even in the face of persecution, were never going to shut their doors. It would be great to know that our evangelistic zeal and love for the neediest has contributed to this open-door commitment.

As we continue to look, we can see that the river of life is in full spate,[234] despite the dams that some within the Church and outside it

---

229. 1 John 2:15-17; James 1:13-15; 2 Corinthians 2:11; Ephesians 6:11.
230. Revelation 21:11,23; 22:5.
231. Revelation 21:14,19.
232. 1 Corinthians 3:12-13.
233. Revelation 21:12,21a,25.
234. Revelation 22:1.

have sought at times to construct to curtail and manage its flow. Every dam and barrier have now been swept aside by the surge of life as the river bounds effervescently onward with sparkling energy. Maybe now is the time to ask ourselves if we are currently in danger of creating dams or barriers that will ultimately need to be removed to release the river in full spate.

And what if we were to look further and focus on the tree of life,[235] flourishing on the banks? Every resident of the city would be able to tell us how at some point in their earthly life they reached out to the 'tree of life' that once stood on a hill called Calvary. Now all of its fruits are constantly available to them, and maybe some of those residents will be there because of conversations they have had with us. And what of the leaves that are carried from the trees by the river of life to bring healing to the nations?[236] Well, nothing in that reality should be a surprise to us. Healing for the nations should have long been high on our agenda.

Eventually, if we were to look down, we would see the transparent streets where the gold glitters through the glass-like surfaces.[237] Oh, for such transparency in our churches today! Oh, for a Church that right now is truly contributing in every way to such a city, adding to the labours of those who have gone before us.

The seven churches in Revelation were promised specific rewards,[238] but in dedicating his whole God-given vision to them, John also set the worshipping host of Revelation 7 and the New Jerusalem of Revelation 21 and 22 before their eyes. These pictures should now be sufficient inspiration for us, even without having to ask our first-century Aegean letter-writers to assign us more specific rewards.

The first-century Church has given us a template for our unity and the book of Revelation has given us a glimpse of its final outcome. Let

---

235. Revelation 22:2a.
236. Revelation 22:2b.
237. Revelation 21:21b.
238. Revelation 2:7b,11b,17b,26-28; 3:5,11-12,21.

us keep reaching out in our different ways until we have gathered people from 'every nation, tribe, people and language'. And let us keep preaching God's Word, maintaining our openness and seeing people renewed by the power of the cross and refreshed by the river of life, as we seek to live with one another in the light of God in absolute transparency.

I believe that with this in mind the whole Church can truly impact society. We have a responsibility to anticipate the ultimate as well as to be real about the immediate. I believe the first-century Church did both and so must we. It grasped the heart of the New Jerusalem and produced something on earth that was real, rugged and robust, without accommodating the slightest hint of superficiality, superiority or sentimentality.

The Church won't be killed by kindness, but we must make sure that there is no misconstrued kindness subverting its mission. God deserves the best from our diversity, and the Holy Spirit is committed to reshaping us, whether by much or by little, so that we can fit together in order to achieve all that God has called us to do.

Postscript

You may not have noticed a short paragraph in my introductory letter, so just in case you missed it, I will share it again here:

This, then, is what this book is about – offering a picture and giving some clear pointers on how the pieces, with God's help, might be able to come together. And so as not to be too ambitious, I am beginning by offering my pointers at a local level.

Actually, there is one sense in which writing at a local level is very ambitious. True, I have chosen not to write a book about national and international Church relations and denominational engagements, partly because at that level I would be addressing relatively few people. What is ambitious here is the belief that change can work upwards; that as church member after church member grasps the need for a more robust expression of unity, there will be a groundswell that will be impossible to ignore. Denominational leaders and governing bodies of churches rightly listen to their local members as they seek the will of God. This is exactly as it should be, since hearing from God in these days of New Covenant grace is not the prerogative of the few. We, as local church members, can read our Bibles, grasp God's Word and express God's heart. We are God's real agents of change. As we live our daily lives in the midst of society, we can support each other.

God's kingdom is made up of individuals rather than power blocks, and we each have a voice. We gather in our local churches and they in turn fit together within God's global plan. Our churches may be grouped denominationally, perhaps having been planted by movements that from the outset had certain distinct principles and historic values in mind. In some cases, they will be upholding a conviction that there should be a single governing body, or hierarchy, to keep everything together. We can respect and understand all of this, but it doesn't take away from the reality of every church member personally being part of *the* Church; a Church that probably God alone, in the fullness of his wisdom, can truly comprehend as it stretches in amazing diversity from the post-ascension Pentecost to the glories in heaven that are yet to come. The unity of the Church is a truth that we have to uphold in the face of all that comes against it. If we recognise how this worked out in the way God wanted it to back in the first century, we will be in a strong position to go forward. Upward pressure works. It did when Antioch referred the circumcision issue to Jerusalem, where it was debated with the unity of the Church in mind. As local church members in local churches, we need to get this kind of practical grassroots unity back at the centre of every national and global Church agenda. I believe it can be done.

The big picture starts with us as church members in our local churches changing things in our towns and villages. News of what we are facing and what we are doing then reaches those with wider influence. It can work. So let's move on from a politely passive kindness for one another and the world around us, and galvanise around a robust and unbreakable love.